Business Law

Business Law

Janice Elliott Montague, MA, LLB, PGCE is Senior Lecturer in Law in the Department of Legal Studies, Coventry Lanchester Polytechnic. She has many years' experience teaching law in further and higher education—particularly to non-lawyers.

Business Law

Janice Elliott Montague

Chambers Commerce Series

Published by W & R Chambers Ltd Edinburgh, 1987

British Library Cataloguing in Publication Data

Montague, Janice Elliott
    Business Law — (Chambers commerce series)
    1. Commercial law — Great Britain
    I. Title
    344.106'7   KD1629
ISBN 0 550 20702 3

Set by Blackwood Pillans & Wilson, Ltd. Edinburgh

Printed in Great Britain by
Richard Clay Ltd,
Bungay, Suffolk

Contents

PART II THE PURCHASE AND SUPPLY OF GOODS AND SERVICES

Chapter 4 Essentials of Contract Law

Chapter 5 The Sale of Goods Act 1979 and The Supply of Goods and Services Act 1982

Chapter 6 Standard-Form Contracts

Chapter 7 Agency

PART IV   THE LAW RELATING TO EMPLOYMENT

Chapter 12   Employing Staff

Chapter 13   Safety at Work

Chapter 14   Dismissal and Redundancy

Preface

This book has been written for those who want to know how the law affects business, whether they are participating in a business studies or other professional course or because they are already working. Although about the law, it is not written for lawyers. It introduces the reader to the role of the law in shaping and influencing business behaviour, explaining important legal concepts in terms understandable to the lay person and correcting some common misconceptions about the law. It is not overburdened with details of cases and statutes, although these have been included where necessary, as the aim throughout has been to relate legal principles to business realities. To this end, subjects are dealt with under practical headings, such as the safety requirements when marketing goods or the effects and meaning of the ubiquitous 'back of order' clauses in contracts.

On finishing this book, the reader will feel better equipped to operate within the business environment through appreciating the legal consequences of her or his actions—at least to know when it might be necessary to consult a lawyer!

The law dealt with is English law, which applies in England and Wales. For reasons explained in Chapter 1, Scottish law is different in both content and procedure, although many modern statutes apply throughout the UK. It has not been possible to deal with the differences in a book of this size and those requiring detailed knowledge of Scottish law are referred to more specialised texts.

Unfamiliar legal terminology has been kept to a minimum, but where it is unavoidable it has been explained where it occurs in the text. Certain other terms which may be unclear to some are printed in italics and appear in a glossary at the end.

I would like to thank several of my colleagues at Coventry Lanchester Polytechnic for their help and also the dozens of business students I have taught over the years, whose irreverence and scepticism about the legal process has kept me on my toes.

This book is dedicated to my father, Anthony Elliott, who has given me the benefit of his experience gained from forty years in the manufacturing trade, and to his grandson, Richard, whose arrival was a very welcome interruption in its preparation.

J.E.M.

PART I

THE BUSINESS ORGANISATION AND ITS LEGAL ENVIRONMENT

Business commentators sometimes argue that one of the problems with the British economy is the excessive number of laws which regulate and hence interfere with the way in which businesses are run. Others recognise that most, if not all, of these laws are helpful in enabling businesses to operate effectively and efficiently, while ensuring that a proper balance is kept between the interests of the businesses, their customers, competitors, creditors and society at large. This book will attempt to show how the most important of these laws operate in practice and why they are thought to be necessary.

Part I gives an outline of the legal environment in which the business must function; the workings of the legal system and the business structures which are recognised and regulated by the law. For more detailed treatment of this area, reference should be made to another book in this series.

Chapter 1

How Laws are Made

As already noted, the commercial and business world is subject to a wide variety of laws. The following chapter deals with the fundamental question of how such laws originate, the ways in which they are made and how businesses can and do influence the form that they take.

1.1 Statute Law

Statute law is the name given to laws made by the body, known as the legislature, which is empowered by the *constitution* of the state to give effect to new laws. In the United Kingdom the legislature is 'the Queen in Parliament', so in other words it is the monarch together with both Houses of Parliament which have the authority to make new laws. Our statute law consists of a large number of Acts of Parliament, or statutes, which are added to, *amended* or *repealed* by each successive government administration. The government, which is made up of members of the majority party in the House of Commons, will introduce legislation to put into effect its political programme, and it is through this process that most new law comes into existence.

To begin with, every new statute is drafted in the form of a bill by parliamentary draftsmen, skilled lawyers who try to ensure that the words used exactly convey the meaning that the government intended. It is these words alone which will be taken as the law and be interpreted by judges and lawyers and followed by civil servants, business people and others. This is why legislation often appears complicated and indeed sometimes incomprehensible to the lay person, but it is intended to be very clear and precise to those who are trained in its use. However, in recent years it has been suggested by such groups as the Plain English Campaign that much current legislation could be written in more straightforward language without losing its precision, thereby making it more accessible to those it is designed to affect.

The bill has to pass through three 'Readings' (which are broadly debates followed by votes) in both the House of Commons and the House of Lords and then be given the Royal Assent before becoming law as an Act of Parliament, although it may not come into force immediately. During this process, amendments may be made to the legislation or whole sections may be altered or abandoned, and it is not unknown for bills to be defeated even when the government has a large majority, especially if there is dissent in the House of Lords. Despite being an unelected body, the House of Lords can play an important role in shaping legislation for, although it has no overall veto, it can delay the process considerably and the government may accept any suggested amendments in order to ensure a smooth passage for its bill.

It is often possible for businesses or industries in Britain acting individually or collectively, through bodies such as the CBI (*Confederation of British Industry*), to influence the final form of the legislation by mobilising political and public opinion during the passage of the bill through Parliament. It is likely that this viewpoint will have already been expressed at an earlier stage anyway, as a result of the involvement of the CBI and others in the political process which influences party policy, or more directly through commenting on government discussion papers, or supplying evidence for Royal Commissions and Committees of Enquiry.

Once enacted, law made by Parliament is sovereign (subject only to EEC law, see Section 1.4) and must be followed by all those to whom it applies, including the *judiciary*. For sanctions against those who do not comply with the law, whether criminal or civil, see Sections 2.1 and 2.2. Acts of Parliament overrule any existing Common Law rule if they are clearly intended to do so, but judges influence the way in which such legislation operates as they have the prime responsibility for interpreting the words of the law. Their interpretation will be binding for the future unless and until Parliament takes action to amend the law. (See further Section 1.3.)

Parliament cannot bind its successors, so any statute can be repealed or amended in the future. On the other hand, all Acts of Parliament however old, outdated and inappropriate they may be, stay in force unless such action is taken, and could conceivably be relied upon in court.

1.2 Delegated Legislation

Some statutes are known as 'enabling Acts' because they only lay down the framework of the law and delegate power to appropriate bodies to make detailed regulations at some later date. This is done because the subject matter of the regulations tends to be very detailed and specialised, and Parliament has neither the time nor the expertise to deal with them all. Authority to make such regulations is often given to the relevant Secretary of State whose department is responsible for the area in question. Examples of this type of legislation which will be considered later are the Health and Safety at Work Act (Section 13.5) and the Consumer Credit Act (Section 11.5). Another illustration of the use of delegated legislative power is the passing of by-laws by local councils under the authority of an Act of Parliament. However, unlike the primary legislation itself, delegated legislation can be challenged in the courts on the grounds that it is *ultra vires* (outside the power of) the body concerned, or that it is unreasonable in scope or effect. (See further Section 2.4.).

In recent years there has been a vast increase in the amount of legislation which has been passed, often to the despair of those who have to keep track of new developments. Copies of statutes and regulations, known as Statutory Instruments, can be obtained from Her Majesty's Stationery Office. However, many laws are not to be found in the statute books at all as they constitute part of the other, and historically more important, form of law in England. This is often called 'judge-made' or 'case' law but is, more accurately, the Common Law.

1.3 Common Law

This form of law may only be familiar to people through reading press references to Common Law wives or husbands, but in fact it is still true that the majority of English rules of law are based on Common Law rather than instigated by Parliament. Areas of law of crucial importance to businesses, such as contract law, are largely composed of Common Law rules (see Chapter 4). This is in contrast to those members of the European Economic Community (EEC) whose laws are contained in written Codes which owe much to ancient Roman Law principles. Former British colonies such as the USA, India and parts of Africa still operate Common Law systems. The fundamental differences between the legal systems goes some way to explain the sometimes uneasy role that the UK plays in the Community! However, many aspects of Scottish law are closer to the continental systems as a result of historical links with France, and this accounts for many of the differences in content and procedure between English and Scottish law.

The Common Law is made up of the decisions of judges over hundreds of years, beginning in Norman times. In an attempt to introduce consistency into a system of law which originated in local customs, the judges have developed a doctrine of *judicial precedent* where similar cases are decided on the same legal principles regardless of how long ago the original case was tried. Whether or not this doctrine applies rigidly depends on the status of the court in which the original decision was made: the more important the court (and sometimes, the judges involved) the greater the requirement to comply with the doctrine and follow the precedent. Any decision made by the House of Lords in its capacity as the highest court in the land will bind itself and all other future courts lower down the hierarchy, except in exceptional circumstances where a future House of Lords may decide that times have changed significantly and overturn its own previous ruling. Any case which reaches the House of Lords, therefore, has a major influence on the way in which the law develops, whether the case involves interpreting a statute, applying a Common Law precedent or a mixture of both. How a case could arrive in the House of Lords will be examined in Section 2.4.

Decisions of lower courts such as the Court of Appeal and the High Court may also create precedents for the future, but are of less authority than those of the House of Lords, and are subject to being overturned by the higher courts or Parliament at a later date. The judgements of these courts are recorded and may be referred to in the appropriate volume of the Law Reports, or frequently nowadays through a computerised data bank retrieval system. The decisions of the lower courts, such as the Crown Court or county courts, do not create precedents and are rarely reported in this way. (See chart for further explanation of the doctrine.)

THE HIERARCHY OF ENGLISH COURTS
Fig. 1   How the Doctrine of Judicial Precedent Works

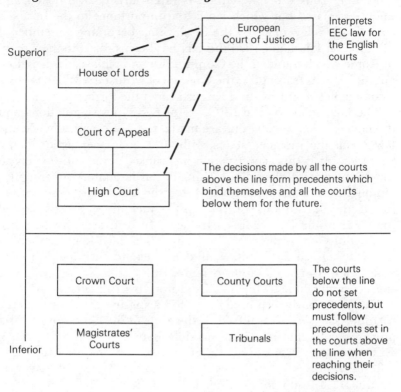

Although 'test cases' are not officially recognised by the English legal system, it is often necessary for a representative action to be taken by an individual or organisation, perhaps backed by a pressure group, to clarify the law in a particular area, e.g. when a new statute is passed or a new situation arises. Others can then rely on this decision with some certainty that in their own case the outcome would be the same if it came to be tried in court. However, as no two situations are ever identical, there is a certain flexibility in the system when circumstances demand. The judge can 'distinguish' a precedent by concentrating on differences between the previous and present cases. Should this be an artificial distinction the losing party would be well advised to appeal, as the decision might then be reversed. (See further Section 2.4.1)

1.4   EEC Law

One other source of law which is often largely overlooked and under-estimated but which is of vital importance to the business community is law made by the EEC. Since becoming a member of the EEC on 1 January 1973 the UK has been subject to the Treaty of Rome which founded the Community and all laws made before and since by its legislature, the Council of Ministers. When there is a conflict between EEC and English Law, the former prevails.

The laws made by the EEC are of two types, regulations and directives. When regulations are made, they automatically become law in all the member states without any further action being necessary. It is this aspect which has caused some controversy in this country about the relinquishing of Parliamentary sovereignty, although it must be remembered that the UK has representatives in all the institutions of the EEC, including directly-elected members of the European Parliament. In contrast, directives are instructions to member states to change their laws to bring them in line with agreed EEC policy, and it is left to each legislature to adapt their own law as appropriate within a time limit. In the UK this is usually done by means of statutory instruments.

Directives have been used to try to harmonise the laws of all the member states in areas affecting the aims of the Community, and an example is that involving product liability (see Section 10.4). EEC law has also had a major impact on the structure and administration of companies (see Chapter 3), equal pay (see Section 12.5), and competition law (see Section 8.9). In the last area the EEC Commission, the administrative branch of the Community, has the power to fine companies up to 10% of their previous year's turnover for breach of the provisions concerning monopolies and cartels, so businesses disregard this EEC law at their peril!

EEC law can in most cases be relied on in the English courts, and the European Court of Justice is only applied to in disputes between member states or the institutions, or for a preliminary interpretation of the law. (See further Section 2.4.)

1.5   Voluntary Law

This name, which may at first sight appear to be a contradiction in terms, has been applied to the increasing use of Codes of Practice as a form of guidance for businesses, rather than reliance on strict, formal law. Such Codes are not enforceable in the courts, but would be used as evidence of good practice if they were complied with. They have been used in particular in relation to employment law and in connection with consumer protection (see Sections 8.5, 12.7, 13.5 and 14.3), and are seen as an important back-up to, but not a substitute for, the legislative framework.

Questions

1 How does a bill become an Act of Parliament?
2 What is the doctrine of judicial precedent?
3 What is meant by the term 'delegated legislation'? Give some examples in your answer. Why is this form of law-making used?
4 Which court in the UK has the power to bind all other courts by its decisions?
5 A decision made by the courts can overrule an Act of Parliament. True or false?
6 What is the difference between an EEC regulation and an EEC directive?
7 Explain briefly the various forms that a new law could take. To what extent could business organisations ensure that their views were taken into account in the formulation of the law?
8 Find out what makes up the current government's legislative programme. Which pieces of legislation are likely to affect businesses? Which bills are going through Parliament at the moment? Who is opposing/supporting this law?

Chapter 2

The English Legal System

A variety of laws provides the framework within which businesses operate on a day-to-day basis, but in many cases they are not conscious of the laws' existence. The following chapter will clarify the different types of law that business is subject to, how the English legal system operates to try to ensure that these laws are complied with and the procedures that are followed when they are not.

2.1   Criminal Law

Some laws proscribe limits over which businesses cannot go, for instance in the amount of polluting substances that can be released into the atmosphere. Others lay down standards that must be met, for example in the amount of information that must be given on food packaging. As these requirements are for the good of the community as a whole, these laws are usually part of the criminal law, which means that if they are broken general disapproval is expressed by regarding these offences as a crime. The criminal process is familiar to most people, if not through personal experience then through the amount of media exposure given to cops-and-robbers stories. However, businesses rarely commit the type of crime that is the stuff of TV drama, and would rarely be prosecuted in the Crown Court where more serious or *indictable* offences are tried by a jury. They are more likely to be tried by lay magistrates by summary procedure in the magistrates' courts for what are often called 'technical offences' under such legislation as the Health and Safety at Work Act (see Section 13.5) and the Trade Descriptions Act (see Section 9.2). Indeed, the vast majority of all criminal cases (approximately 98%) are dealt with in this manner.

The most common punishment for such business offences is a fine, because it is obviously not possible to imprison a company, nor sentence it to do community service, unless the offence 'was committed by a sole trader (see Section 3.1), or an individual employee can be held to be personally responsible. The threat of possibly incurring such a penalty goes some way to explain how the criminal law is imposed. In the case of a business, the need to avoid the resultant bad publicity from a conviction is probably an even more compelling incentive.

Most crimes are detected by the police, but in the case of businesses the investigators and enforcers are more likely to be other public officials, such as Factory Inspectors, Trading Standards Officers and the like. Even when offences are detected, the authorities will very often prefer to warn the business concerned rather than prosecute. Obviously, it is more satisfactory to ensure that the standards are reached and the harmful activities prevented than to engage in a costly and lengthy trial at public expense, although this may sometimes be necessary to deter a persistent offender or to warn other traders who may be tempted to transgress.

In summary, therefore, the criminal law is used to try to mould behaviour into an approved pattern. It is sometimes argued that it is an inappropriate tool to use in regulating businesses, as the type of behaviour involved is somehow not 'wicked' enough to be branded as criminal, and that some other method of penalising undesirable business behaviour should be introduced. Much of the thinking behind this is prompted by the suspicion that many unscrupulous businesses regard the periodical imposition of relatively light fines as part of their expected business overheads. It is felt that another system, divested of the stigma of the criminal law, could impose more realistic penalties, such as publishing corrections of misleading information.

2.2 Civil Law

Although not as visible as the criminal law, the majority of laws that regulate business activities are part of the civil law. This is the general term given to the laws which govern the rights and obligations owed by each member of the community to each other. Some civil law duties are voluntarily undertaken, for instance entering into a contract or getting married, while others are simply essential to allow for peaceful co-existence and interaction between individuals. An example of this latter type of obligation is the duty which exists to take reasonable care for those who, it can be foreseen, could be harmed if the activity was carried out without that degree of care. When that duty is not fulfilled, and someone is injured as a result, the *tort* of negligence has been committed. The injured party may then claim compensation from the person who committed the tort. This person will be the defendant in the ensuing action if the matter is not settled out of court, which is more usual (see Section 2.5).

This is the essence of the civil law – it is left to the individual party (known as the plaintiff) to take action on her or his own behalf to remedy the wrong whether they be an individual or organisation. The only remedy that the legal system can realistically provide in most cases is money to compensate, as far as possible, for the harm suffered. So, if a contractual obligation is broken, the ultimate remedy for the affected party is to sue in the civil courts for money compensation known as damages. (For other remedies which are sometimes available see Section 4.11). The purpose of this is not to punish the wrongdoer, but to compensate the wronged.

Partly as a result of this liability businesses will generally seek to abide by their obligations, although another important factor is undoubtedly the need to preserve and enhance a good reputation. Very often the threat of *litigation* will be enough to ensure that the obligation is met, or that an 'out-of-court' settlement can be reached – see Section 2.5. But such a threat will be hollow if the defendant is 'a man of straw', i.e. without resources, such as a company in liquidation or a person whose property is all in his spouse's name. Even if the action is successful, the plaintiff can recover from the defendant only. If there are no assets belonging to the defendant that can be easily realised, the plaintiff will have no remedy. Companies sometimes try to avoid the consequences of this by attempting to retain rights over goods supplied to a customer, but this is not always successful (see further Section 6.7).

Knowing that these laws exist enables businesses to operate with the certainty that, provided they act in a particular way, the outcome will be as they intend. They can draw up contracts in a manner which will serve their purposes, protect their products and inventions by means of trade marks and patents, calculate their insurance cover against potential liability to pay compensation to customers, employees and others, and otherwise regulate their relationships and organise their affairs in a satisfactory manner. Only as a last resort will it be necessary to assert these rights in court. In the vast majority of cases no dispute will arise as a result of complying with the law. If a dispute does arise, it can be settled by simply applying the correct principles of law. (See further Section 2.5 below.)

2.3 The Relationship between Civil and Criminal Law

An important point to clarify is that both the civil law and criminal law are made up partly of statutes and partly of Common Law precedents. For example, although, as has already been mentioned, contract law is primarily based on cases, there are also statutes such as the Sale of Goods Act and the Unfair Contract Terms Act which regulate certain aspects of this area of law (see Chapters 4, 5 and 6). Indeed, some pieces of legislation, such as the former, are only a *codification* of old Common Law principles, while others like the latter are entirely new reforms made by Parliament.

Another fundamental point which sometimes causes confusion is that the same set of circumstances can involve both the civil and the criminal law. For example, if a manufacturer produces a commodity which does not comply with safety regulations made under the Consumer Safety Act (see Section 10.7), the manufacturer will have committed a criminal offence for which it may be prosecuted by the state in the criminal courts and punished, probably by way of a fine, if found guilty. Additionally, an injured consumer of the product could seek compensation from the supplier to cover the cost of medical expenses, loss of earnings, etc. incurred as a result. In theory two separate actions in the two court systems would be necessary, as explained below. In practice, if there was a successful prosecution, the company concerned would probably settle with the consumer to avoid further expense and the inevitable adverse publicity of further court proceedings. There is, of course, no opportunity to settle criminal proceedings once they have been instituted, unless the judge decides insufficient evidence exists to proceed.

Sometimes the criminal law is used to try to strengthen the effects of the civil law, so that the two systems are complementary. This may be necessary where, for example, the civil provisions are not widely appreciated by the public and are therefore not invoked, whereas the appropriate state official is under a duty to enforce the criminal law. For example, it is an offence to purport to exclude certain inalienable rights from contracts which are guaranteed by the civil law (see Section 5.4).

2.4   The Courts

As mentioned above, the two systems of law have separate court systems to deal with disputes. In the case of the criminal law, the courts of first instance (i.e. where the case is heard for the first time) are the magistrates and the Crown Court, with appeals possible usually to the Court of Appeal, against conviction or the penalty imposed, and ultimately, if there is a point of law of fundamental importance to be settled, to the House of Lords (see chart below).

The civil courts of first instance are the county courts and the High Court. Businesses are likely to find themselves involved in county court proceedings in cases concerning broken contracts, debts and claims for damages of less than £5000 or hire purchase repossessions. Such cases are dealt with by a single judge and no jury. Claims for under £500 are dealt with on a relatively informal basis, without the need for legal representation, by a registrar in

THE ENGLISH COURTS
Fig. 2a   The Criminal Courts

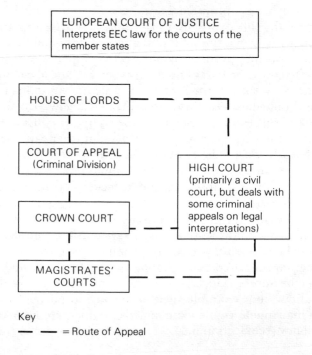

Fig. 2b   The Civil Courts

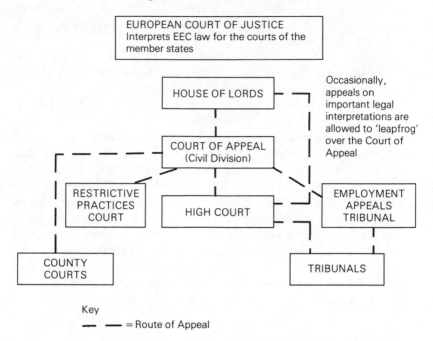

private. This procedure for small claims was introduced in 1973 to help individuals assert their rights and has meant that a threat to sue for a comparatively small sum is now more realistic and therefore should be taken more seriously than might previously have been the case.

The High Court is divided into three divisions of which the Queen's Bench Division (QBD) is of most interest to businesses. This is the busiest of the divisions and deals with all claims for breach of contract or for personal injuries of over £5000 with no top limit. A commercial court with more specialised judges sits to deal with commercial matters. The Chancery Division is concerned with tax and trust matters, and includes a specialised companies court and patents court. The Family Division, as the name implies, deals with family problems. The QBD also sits as a court of appeal, when by a process known as judicial review it can re-examine and perhaps quash decisions of government departments.

Appeals are possible, provided the means are available, to the Court of Appeal consisting of three judges, and thence to the House of Lords for a final appeal in front of, usually, five judges.

Again this is only possible if an important point of law is at stake and, as in the criminal system, leave to appeal must be obtained. (It may be possible to 'leap-frog' over the Court of Appeal in some cases – see chart above).

The House of Lords is therefore the highest court of appeal in the English legal system. Appeal may be possible to the European Court of Justice, but only where a point of EEC law is involved, and even then the final decision is made by the English courts on the basis of the Court's interpretation. A distinction must be drawn between this Court and the European Court of Human Rights to which appeals may be made as a last resort if it is felt that the European Convention of Human Rights has been breached.

The cost of taking a case as far as the House of Lords may well run into tens of thousands of pounds, taking into account court and lawyers' fees and the normal practice of making the loser pay all of the winner's costs as well. Another cost which cannot be ignored when contemplating legal action is time, as top personnel may be involved in such a case for many years. It is for this reason that legal action should be avoided if at all feasible by obtaining good legal advice both before and after a dispute arises. (See Section 2.8.)

2.5   Out-of-Court Settlements

Because of the cost and time involved in taking a case to court, the majority of civil cases are settled before going to trial. The two parties reach some compromise agreement between themselves at any stage before or during court proceedings. In fact some cases are settled literally at the door of the court on the day of the hearing, because both parties will have been negotiating over many months to achieve the best possible solution for themselves, and the one that has been advised that it has the weaker case will finally come to terms. It is therefore only the rare and slightly unusual case that gets to the stage of court proceedings, in situations where neither side can be certain of the legal position or a complicated question of fact has to be decided.

2.6   Arbitration

Another reason why many civil disputes are not aired in open court is that businesses often prefer their disputes to be settled by way of arbitration. This would involve appointing a mutually acceptable third party, the arbitrator, to decide on the matter, in effect 'privatising' the functions of the courts and the judiciary. The advantages of this course of action are as follows.

First, the chosen arbitrator will almost certainly be an expert in the subject at the heart of the dispute and will be in a position to judge the worth of the opposing arguments without a great deal of explanation, whilst still reaching a decision based on the law. The disputing parties may well, therefore, have more faith in the decision than one made by an expert solely or mainly in the law, and the whole proceedings can be disposed of more quickly. Second, the parties can choose not only the arbitrator, but also when and where the case can be heard for their convenience, rather than wait for a time and place to be allocated by the court. The arbitration will almost certainly be arranged as a private hearing, without press or public present, which means that no adverse publicity will be generated, nor commercial secrets aired.

It used to be argued that an arbitration was much cheaper than going to court, but this has been questioned lately because lawyers are usually still a necessity and arbitrators can command very high fees. Also, if the case goes from arbitration on appeal to the courts then another tier has simply been added to the existing court system. However, since the Arbitration Act 1979, which along with the Arbitration Acts 1950 and 1975 controls the conduct of arbitration, it has become more difficult to appeal to the courts from the award of the arbitrator as both parties or one party and the court has to agree it is necessary as a point of law is in doubt. It is even possible to exclude the possibility of an appeal at all, so that the arbitrator's award is final and binding. (See further Section 6.8).

Many companies put arbitration clauses into their contracts as a matter of course and this, coupled with the propensity to settle cases on the basis of their tightly drawn contracts, means that fewer commercial cases than previously appear in the courts and therefore fewer commercial precedents are set. This has led some commentators to question whether the law as it stands today is altogether a true reflection of business realities.

This use of the term arbitration must be distinguished from two other methods of dispute resolution that may be familiar to business people – ACAS (Advisory, Conciliation and Arbitration Service) and the small-claims procedure. Arbitration is one of the functions of the government agency ACAS, which can be called upon to try to settle industrial relations disputes between employers and their employees. (See further Section 12.8.) Under the small-claims procedure in the county court, an arbitrator will decide claims of under £500 (see Section 2.4 above), but of course this is part of the state system and so the parties do not choose their own arbitrator.

London is an important centre for international commercial arbitrations and this explains why cases with unpronounceable names and seemingly little connection with Britain sometimes appear in the Law Reports as a result of appeals from the arbitrator's award.

2.7   Tribunals

Another feature of the English legal system in recent years is the growing number of tribunals which have been set up to deal with disputes. Tribunals range from the formal Lands Tribunal to the supposed informality of the Supplementary Benefits Appeals Tribunals, but the characteristics that they share are that, unlike courts, they specialise in one particular aspect of law and the members of the tribunal will include experts as well as lawyers.

The tribunals with which businesses are most likely to come into contact are industrial tribunals, which deal with the rights of employees concerning unfair dismissal and redundancy, etc. (See further Part IV.) Each tribunal is made up of a legal chairperson and a representative from a local panel of employers and a similar representative from the workers' side of industry. The proceedings are more informal than a court and lawyers are discouraged from attending, although both parties are often represented, perhaps by a trade union representative or personnel officer. One consequence of this discouragement is that Legal Aid, which is usually available to help individuals pay their legal fees, is not granted for tribunal hearings.

2.8   Lawyers

Many larger companies will employ lawyers on their staff to advise on the legal consequences of their operations, but smaller businesses will need to consult external firms as necessary. In-house lawyers may have qualified as barristers or solicitors, but when consulting externally it will be necessary to contact a firm of solicitors as it is not possible to approach practising barristers directly. England and Wales retain this split in the legal profession, which does not exist in Scotland, and this difference sometimes causes confusion. Solicitors are best regarded as the GPs of the profession, although increasingly nowadays firms are beginning to specialise in one or two aspects of law. It is as well to check before engaging a solicitor as to whether the firm is experienced in commercial matters. Barristers on the other hand specialise in one field such as tax law. They are available to give 'counsel's opinion' to solicitors needing to advise clients how to proceed in a complex matter, or to represent these clients in the higher courts, as solicitors at present have no rights of audience there. However, solicitors can and do carry out all the groundwork preparation and negotiating in a case. Very often the case can be settled following an exchange of letters, without a court hearing and without having to engage a barrister at all.

Questions

1 Explain the difference between the functions and procedures of the criminal and civil law in England and Wales.
2 Why do some businesses prefer to have their disputes settled by arbitration rather than use the court system?
3 How do tribunals differ from the ordinary courts? Give examples of the names and functions of tribunals that you know of.
4 Where could the following cases be heard:
   (a) a claim for breach of contract involving damages of £15000?
   (b) a breach of the Trade Descriptions Act?
   (c) a claim to repossess hire purchase goods by a finance house?
   (d) a serious tax fraud?
   (e) a dispute between two businesses in which one is claiming payment of a debt of £1700 and the other is counter-claiming for damages of £600?
5 Explain the different services provided to businesses by solicitors and barristers in England and Wales.
6 What factors would have to be taken into account when deciding whether to sue another business? What other alternatives would be open to you?

7 One of your employees is badly injured as a result of slipping on the factory floor which had not been properly cleaned after a spillage of oil. You have been informed that there may have been a breach of the Health and Safety at Work Act and that the employee is claiming compensation for her injuries on the ground of your negligence. Explain who would initiate the case, how it would be dealt with and the likely outcome if your company loses the case.

Chapter 3
Forms of Business Organisation

Businesses can set themselves up in a variety of ways and the form that they take depends on a number of factors – commercial, financial and legal. This chapter will identify the legal implications associated with operating as a sole trader, a partnership or a limited company and will briefly examine the attractions and drawbacks of each form.

3.1 Sole Traders

Apart from particular types of business which require prior authorisation by way of the grant of a licence (e.g. those supplying credit, see Section 11.6, or alcohol to consumers) most businesses can be started up by an individual with little or no formality, provided that obligations such as planning controls and taxation are taken into account. It is no longer necessary to register the name of a business, but if a name other than the proprietor's is chosen to operate under, then the name and address of the owner must be displayed on the business premises and stationery and this information must be supplied on request. Use of an unsuitable name, such as one that is too similar to an existing business, can be prohibited.

Sole traders do not need to be a 'one-man business' as they can and do employ staff. The advantages of operating in this way are that all the decisions and ultimately the profits are the owner's, but of course this is coupled with sole responsibility and the fact that all the liabilities of the business are personal debts. Unlike companies (see Section 3.3 below) the law does not regard the business as separate in any way from the owner. It is for this reason and because of the need to expand and have extra capital that people are encouraged to set up their businesses as companies.

21

3.2   Partnerships

A stage in between a sole trader and a company, which can introduce new capital and expertise into the business without too much expense and formality, is to organise the business as a partnership, i.e. to take in other people as part-owners of the enterprise. Again it is possible to do this without any legal formalities, although it is normally considered advisable to draw up a deed of partnership at the outset to clarify the main features of the arrangement, such as the division of profits and so on. It is also necessary to comply with the requirements about the business name as in the case of a sole trader. Although partners are perfectly at liberty to define their relationship as they choose, if this has not been expressly set out then the Partnership Act 1890 will apply. This defines a partnership as 'the relationship which subsists between persons carrying on a business in common with a view to profit', and thus an arrangement that has these characteristics may be deemed to exist as a partnership even if the individuals concerned do not see themselves as such. The maximum number of partners allowed is twenty, except in the case of certain professional partnerships, such as accountants and solicitors, which are not allowed to form companies. Technically, the collective term for the partnership entity is the firm, although some people refer to all business enterprises in this manner.

The legal position of the partnership is that each partner is jointly liable for all contracts entered into by any partner on behalf of the firm. This means that each individual partner is personally liable, with the others, for the firm's debts to the limits of their private resources, even if they did not know about the contracts when they were made. In circumstances where the firm commits a tort in the course of the business, perhaps by giving negligent advice, all the partners are 'jointly and severally' liable, which means they can be held individually liable to pay compensation from their personal assets. In effect, the partners are acting as agents for each other (see further Chapter 7) and this is why it is essential for there to be a close and trusting relationship between partners.

When this trust breaks down, or partners wish to leave the business for some other reason, the partnership may have to be dissolved and, if the business wishes to continue, it has to be reorganised. A retiring partner should ensure that all previous contacts are notified so that he or she is not held liable in the future for activities of the firm, and ensure that his or her name is erased from letterheadings, etc. The bankruptcy or death of a partner will also bring a partnership to an end unless it has been otherwise agreed.

Occasionally, limited partnerships are formed where 'sleeping partners' contribute capital but play no part in the running of the business and are not liable for the debts of the firm. However, these partnerships have to register details with the Registrar of Companies. They are somewhat rare as it is almost as easy to form a limited company (see below). But they do share with all other firms the advantage over companies of not having to disclose their accounts.

3.3   Companies

In the nineteenth century it became apparent that in order for business enterprises to grow they required to have large numbers of investors. It was equally clear that people were reluctant to put money into a business over which they had little direct control but for whose debts they would be personally responsible. A process known as incorporation was therefore developed, which allowed a separate legal entity, the corporation or company, to be created, in which the owners' liability could be limited.

Most companies today are incorporated under the procedure laid down in the Companies Act 1985, with the shareholders' liability limited to the nominal value of their shares (i.e. the amount originally promised in return for their allotment).

Apart from this limited liability of the shareholders, the other major attraction of companies as a form of business organisation is that once created, the company is seen as a separate legal 'person' with rights and liabilities of its own, distinct from the members. This feature was confirmed by the House of Lords in *Salomon* v *Salomon & Co. Ltd.* [1897] A.C. 22* where a shoemaker called Salomon sold his business to a company with himself and his family as the only shareholders. He then lent the company some money. When the business failed, Salomon claimed he was entitled to be paid as a preferential creditor before all the other creditors. The others naturally challenged this, pointing out that Salomon and Salomon and Co. were in reality the same thing. The courts

* The reference (or 'citation') following the names of cases denotes the law report in which the full judgements can be found in a Law Library.

held, however, that the company had acquired a separate legal 'personality' from Salomon through the process of incorporation and therefore Salomon was entitled to be repaid first. The company was not merely an alias or agent for Salomon.

It is therefore important to remember that every business that operates as a company has this unique attribute, and that it is the *company* that owns property, makes contracts on its own behalf, can sue in its own name or commit crimes – *not* the shareholders, directors or employees. The company operates as a completely distinct entity from the humans who own and control it, and will continue to operate even when the owners or managers change. In the event of the company ceasing to operate, its debts belong to no-one but the company itself, and if the company's assets are not enough to cover its liabilities then no other person is responsible for them save in exceptional circumstances. (See further Sections 3.5 and 11.1). It is in return for the privileges of limited liability and separate legal personality, and to protect those who deal with companies, that extra controls and obligations are placed on companies, as shown in Section 3.5 below.

Although it has been said that most commercial enterprises operate as companies limited by shares, some business organisations such as workers' co-operatives are companies limited by guarantee, which means that the extent of each member's liability (in this case, the employees') is limited to the amount of the guarantee.

3.4   Public and Private Limited Companies

Companies limited by shares come in two forms, public and private. The main characteristic of a public company is that it has to allot at least £50000 of shares, of which at least one-quarter are fully paid-up (i.e. have been paid for in full by the shareholders). These companies must include the words 'public limited company' (plc) at the end of their name and it must be clearly stated in the memorandum of association (see below) that the company is public. All other companies are private. The main difference between the two is that private companies cannot offer their shares to the general public, but retain control over who can be a shareholder. Public companies do not have this limitation and some (but not all) are listed on, and have their shares dealt in by, the Stock Exchange. They tend therefore to be the larger companies, but most companies in this country are private companies often owned and controlled by one family.

The other major difference between the two is that smaller private companies do not have to disclose as much information in their published accounts. Both types of companies must have a minimum of two members but there is no longer any maximum number.

3.5   The 'Life and Death' of a Company

Companies are created through the process of incorporation. This involves drawing up two main documents, the memorandum and articles of association. The memorandum deals with the external affairs of the company such as its name, registered office, purpose or objects, share capital, etc. The articles deal with the internal running of the company, such as the rights of shareholders at meetings and the directors' powers. A standard set of articles which are laid down in the Companies Act may be used.

These documents, along with others dealing with the amount of capital and the directors' names, are submitted with the appropriate fee to the Registrar of Companies who then issues a certificate of incorporation if all is in order. Private companies can then begin trading, while public companies must further satisfy the Registrar that the necessary share capital has been allotted before doing so. These details are open for public inspection on the register held at Companies House in Cardiff.

A company can only carry out activities that come within the objects clause in its memorandum of association. This is known as the company's 'capacity' and is dealt with in detail later (Section 4.8). If necessary, the objects clause can be changed in accordance with the procedure laid down in the Companies Act 1985.

The 1985 Act regulates the conduct of a company's affairs in so far as it must regularly prepare and publish information about its activities for its shareholders and others such as creditors, hold meetings and maintain registers of its members. Companies are thus more closely controlled and regulated by outsiders than the other forms of business organisations considered in this chapter. In theory the shareholders 'own' the company but in practice day-to-day management is in the hands of the directors, who are responsible to the company as a whole. The board of directors acts as the human agent of the company (see further, Chapter 7). A public company has a minimum of two directors, while a private company need only have one, plus a company secretary.

The company can continue trading until it is either compulsorily or voluntarily wound up by the members or creditors. This normally happens if the company is in financial difficulties. The assets of the company are gathered together by the person appointed as liquidator and then as many as possible of the debts are paid off, with tax arrears and employees' pay at the top of the list and unsecured creditors (usually other traders) at the bottom. Once the assets of the company, including the full nominal value of the shares, have been dispersed, neither the directors nor shareholders have any personal liability for the debts and these will remain unpaid, except in rare instances where fraudulent or wrongful trading is involved.

Questions

1 What factors influence the choice of structure for the operation of a business?
2 What is the maximum number of partners in a partnership?
3 Explain the meaning of the following terms:
   (a) plc
   (b) certificate of incorporation
   (c) winding up a company
   (d) limited liability.
4 Explain the importance of the decision in *Salomon* v *Salomon & Co. Ltd.*
5 What is the difference between:
   (a) public and private companies?
   (b) memorandum and articles of association?
6 Find out as much as possible about the way the Stock Exchange works (e.g. see other books in this series.)

   Choose a couple of companies whose shares you would like to buy and follow their progress over a couple of months. How would you find out about the companies' activities and the factors affecting the share price?
7 Do you think that all employees should own shares in the company for which they work? What would be the implications of this?

PART II

THE PURCHASE AND SUPPLY OF GOODS AND SERVICES

Business activity generally involves the buying and selling of commodities, be they goods or services, to other businesses or to the general public. This Part will examine the role of the law in facilitating these transactions by providing a framework of rules within which business and commerce may operate.

Chapter 4

Essentials of Contract Law

The basic exchange that is a necessary part of the process of sale is governed and facilitated by the Law of Contract. In this chapter we examine the rules which the courts have evolved over the years to enable contracts to be recognised and enforced.

4.1 What is Meant by a 'Contract'?

A contract is nothing more nor less than a legally binding agreement, i.e. one that the courts will enforce. Generally, there is no necessity for the contract to be in any particular form such as in writing, and indeed the vast majority of contracts are made orally in everyday life when, for example, buying goods in shops or boarding a bus. It is rarely necessary for these contracts to be enforced, but if they were the procedure would be the same. The person who claimed that the contract had not been properly fulfilled, i.e. breached, would have to seek compensation in the form of damages.

But as Samuel Goldwyn is reputed to have said, 'An oral contract is not worth the paper it is written on'. Therefore most contracts between businesses *are* in writing because it is then obviously easier to prove that the contract was made and what terms were decided upon. However, as will be seen, it is not always clear which terms do govern the contract in question, as various documents and lengthy negotiations may have surrounded the moment of agreement, which is what the courts would try to identify. It is not necessary, and often not possible, to identify just one document that constitutes the contract, as its terms may be contained in various letters, telexes and other documents. See Section 4.5 below.

Over the years that the courts developed the Common Law rules governing the law of contract, the fundamental principle that was

29

borne in mind was that of freedom of contract. This meant that the courts were prepared to enforce any agreement that was made between the parties, provided only that it conformed with the characteristics of a contract. The judges were not concerned with the content of the contract, only its structure. It was felt that persons should be free to make any bargain, and that the courts should not interfere in this process. In recent years with the development of standard-form contracts, and the growth of huge commercial conglomerates, this idea of an equally negotiated and freely entered agreement has become increasingly unrealistic. Parliament has therefore had to step in to protect the consumer and the small business person in this process.

However, it is still true that the vast majority of contract law is judge-made, dating from the era of industrial expansion in the nineteenth century, and it therefore sometimes sits somewhat uneasily in present-day commercial conditions. But if businesses wish to take advantage of the protection afforded by the law of contract then it is necessary that they understand what the legal concept of a contract entails. Businesses may not wish to enforce their strict legal rights under a contract for reasons of business expediency, but will still wish to make use of the contractual device for the purposes of pricing and certainty of outcome, with the option of enforcing their agreement if need be. Additionally it means that a settlement can be negotiated from a position of strength once the legal position is established.

In order for the courts to recognise an agreement as a contract, and be prepared to enforce it, the agreement must have three basic characteristics: the parties must have intended the agreement to be legally binding, there must have been a clear offer that has been fully accepted (i.e. agreement between the parties has been reached), and there must be an element of consideration. The courts will not enforce a gratuitous promise. The questions that are asked to determine if each of these elements exists will be examined in turn.

4.2   Did the Parties Intend to Be Legally Bound?

It is not necessary for intending contracting parties to express their desire to be legally bound in so many words, as in business situations the courts assume that such an intention exists, unless strong evidence can be shown to the contrary. However, in social or domestic situations the courts assume the opposite to be true, so in order for such an agreement to be binding there must exist strong evidence that the parties so intended.

Several cases involving football pools companies illustrate that it is possible to make a gentleman's agreement in a business situation, although whether the plaintiffs in the cases would have described the situation in such terms is questionable. In *Appleson* v *Littlewoods Limited* [1939] 1 All E.R. 464 it has been held that the words 'this agreement is binding in honour only' printed on the forms was sufficient to rebut the presumption in favour of the binding nature of the agreement, and thus the disappointed jackpot winners could not sue for breach of contract when their claims to be paid were not met. Obviously the pools companies only rely on this clause in extreme cases, as they would not remain in business very long if they continually refused to pay out!

If a contract exists it is not possible to exclude the *jurisdiction* of the courts from dealing with it, except in limited circumstances when an arbitration clause is invoked (see Section 6.8). If no contract exists at all then this may be achieved as in *Rose & Frank* v *Crompton Brothers* [1925] A.C. 445 where a clause stating 'this arrangement is not entered into as a formal or legal agreement and shall not be subject to legal jurisdiction in the Law Courts' was sufficient to preclude the agreement from being regarded as a contract.

Agreements made between Trade Unions and employers are, contrary to the usual business situation, deemed not to be legally binding unless expressly stated to be so, which occurs only very rarely. This means that breach of a collective agreement cannot be sued upon in the courts by either side, unless the agreement is expressly or by implication incorporated into individual employees' contracts of employment (see further Section 12.3).

4.3 Has a True Offer Been Made?

During the process of negotiations there will usually come a point where one party makes an offer which, if accepted by the other party, can be said to constitute agreement. The courts have to have rules to establish when such an offer has been made, as it may not always be clear. In certain instances where it may appear an offer has been made, the courts have held that the parties are still in the preliminary stages before an offer and therefore no contract can have come into existence.

(a) Is the offer merely an 'invitation to treat'?

When goods are displayed in shop windows or in stores or as part of advertisements or catalogues, with or without price tickets and regardless of such additional frills as placards stating that they are offers or special offers, courts have decided that only an invitation to treat has been made. In other words, such displays are inviting the other party to make an offer to buy, and sellers are therefore in a position to reject or accept such offer as they choose.

The same reasoning can be applied to price lists, asking for tenders or quotes to be submitted, and auction sales when the auctioneer requests bids to be made. In all these situations, then, it is the person who responds who is held to be the *offeror*. Although the other party can and frequently will accept this offer, there is no obligation to do so, and it therefore cannot be relied upon.

This is a general statement of the rule and each case will be decided on the precise wording used. Two major exceptions should be pointed out. The first is that it is possible to phrase an advertisement in such a manner that the court would be prepared to hold that an offer to the whole world has been made, and that simply by carrying out the terms of the advertisement a contract has been formed. This is shown in the well-known case of *Carlill* v *The Carbolic Smoke Ball Company* [1893] 1 Q.B. 256, where the company published an advertisement which promised £100 (and in 1893 £100 was a lot of money!) to anyone who sniffed their smoke ball but still contracted 'flu. They were so convinced of their product's effectiveness that they also stated that they had deposited £1000 in a bank account to substantiate their claim. Mrs Carlill used the smoke ball as instructed but still caught 'flu. She had to take the case as far as the Court of Appeal before she received the promised payment. This decision helps to explain why such precise and well-documented claims are rarely seen in today's advertisements (see further Chapter 9).

Similarly, where it is made absolutely clear that the highest bid or the lowest tender of quotes will be accepted, then the party who submits it should be able to maintain that a contract has been concluded. This was held in the case of *Harvela Investments Ltd* v *Royal Trust Company of Canada* [1985] 1 All E.R. 261 where there were only two possible bidders and it was explicitly stated that the highest bid would be accepted.

(b) Is the offer merely the provision of information?

It was held in *Harvey* v *Facey* [1893] A.C. 552 that the statement in response to an enquiry that the lowest price to be accepted was £900 did not constitute an offer and could not therefore be said to bind the provider of that information. However, again, the decision may well depend on the exact wording of the document and the actions of the parties involved, who may be held to be making a definite offer.

(c) Is the offer merely a letter of intent?

Such a letter may be regarded as a step in negotiations before a final offer has been made, expressing as it does the intention of the party to make an offer at some later time, but perhaps instructing the other party to begin work in the meantime. It may lead to the situation where all the work is completed on the basis of the letter and other continuing negotiations without a contract ever having been made. This was the case in *British Steel Corporation* v *Cleveland Bridge Engineering Co. Ltd.* [1984] 1 All E.R. 504 where the court held that, as such basic points as the price and other specifications had never been finally settled between the parties, no contract had ever come into existence and payment for the work done could not be calculated on the basis of either party's written terms on which no agreement had been reached. But the court conceded in the course of the judgement that letters of intent could form the basis of a contract if all that was required was acting on that letter to be taken to have accepted a full, clearly expressed offer. The wording of such documents will therefore again be of vital importance.

4.4 Is the Offer Still in Existence When It Is Accepted by the Other Party?

Once an offer is made, it can come to an end in a number of ways and then can no longer be accepted and form a contract.

Offers which are made for a fixed term will automatically end at the expiry of that time. But even if the period has not fully elapsed, the offeror can withdraw the offer at any time before it is accepted, because the promise to keep the offer open for, say, six weeks is not supported by consideration. It is therefore usual in the business context to 'buy an option' which will guarantee that the offer is left open and, if it is not, that the offeror can be sued for breach of the secondary, option contract. The price paid for the option ensures that the promise is supported by consideration and is therefore binding. See Section 4.7 below.

The time at which the cancellation or revocation is effective may also be important – see Section 4.6 below.

In the situation where no limit is placed on the length of time in which the offer will remain open, then it will lapse automatically after a reasonable time. What is reasonable will depend on the circumstances of the case – an offer to sell perishable foodstuffs will obviously lapse before an offer to sell hard-wearing goods.

The original offer also ends if a counter-offer is made as in *Hyde* v *Wrench* [1840] 3 Beav. 334, where the original offer to sell a farm for £1000 was met by a counter-offer for a price of £950. This brought the original offer to an end, and the prospective buyer could not re-instate the original offer and insist the farm was sold to him at £1000. This rule that a new offer extinguishes the original one and substitutes itself as the offer has led to difficulties associated with the modern practice of using sets of standard terms on which to contract. See below.

4.5   Has an Unqualified Acceptance of the Offer Occurred?

At the point where an unqualified, full acceptance of a true offer takes place, agreement has been reached and from that moment (provided that the parties intend to be bound and an element of consideration is present) a contract has been made and the parties are bound.

However, sometimes the offeree may appear to be accepting the offer but is trying to introduce new terms or conditions into the agreement. In effect this would amount to a counter-offer. Therefore, as in the case of *Northland Airliners Limited* v *Denis Ferranti Masters Limited, The Times*, 23 October 1970, where a cable was sent by sellers 'confirming sale to you G.M. Aircraft . . . please remit £5000' and the reply was 'This is to confirm your cable and my purchase G.M. Aircraft terms set out your cable . . . £5000 Sterling forwarded your bank to be held in trust for your account pending delivery . . . Please confirm delivery to be made 30 days within this date', the original offeror was not bound to fulfil the order as the reply did not constitute an acceptance in full of the offer.

The 'Battle of the Forms'

This term is used to describe the situation where both parties attempt to enter an agreement on the basis of their own standard terms and conditions. It is highly unlikely that the two sets of terms will correspond with one another: for instance a seller is likely to include a price variation clause where a buyer is likely to state that the quoted price is final. Therefore, if an offer to sell is made on the seller's standard form and the buyer purportedly accepts this on a form which includes different terms, then applying the rule in *Hyde v Wrench*, the seller's terms have been rejected by the buyer's counter-offer. If the seller then continues with the order the courts are likely to decide that by implication the seller has accepted the buyer's terms. This has been termed the 'last shot doctrine' as the party whose terms are sent last will see his prevail. This was illustrated in *British Road Services* v *Arthur Crutchley & Co. Ltd.* [1968] 1 All E.R. 811 where the last shot was in fact the overstamping of the goods received note with a rubber stamp which stated 'accepted on our terms and conditions'. The entire contract was held to have been entered into on these terms.

However, before it can be said that either side has accepted the terms by implication by carrying through the agreement, either side will be able to withdraw without fear of being in breach, as no contract will have been made – see the *Northland Airliners* case above. But once any work has been carried out the courts will be very reluctant to say no contract has been concluded. However, if this is an inescapable conclusion, the party who has performed under the agreement will be entitled to receive a reasonable sum for his work, but not what was suggested in the proposed contract, as in the *Cleveland Bridge* case, above.

Lord Denning in *Butler Machine Tool Co. Ltd.* v *Ex-Cell-O Corporation (England) Limited* [1979] 1 All E.R. 965 tried to introduce a more realistic analysis of the position when confronted with a battle of the forms. The sellers, after an exchange of conflicting documents, finally sent a tear-off acknowledgement slip from the buyer's order form which stated that the order was accepted on the buyer's terms. They then tried to argue that an accompanying letter which referred to their own quotation on their terms should be regarded as 'the last shot' but Lord Denning looked at the arrangement as a whole and concluded that the buyer's terms prevailed. His other two colleagues in the Court of Appeal (and therefore the majority) although reaching the same conclusion, used the traditional analysis of offer, counter-offer, acceptance, and so this is likely to continue when such problems confront the court.

It is likely that many everyday business transactions technically do not constitute contracts, but provided both sides think they know what was agreed and this is identical or can be negotiated away, then no problem arises. However, if the agreement has to be analysed by the courts, it will be subjected to the application of these rules in order to arrive at a conclusion about whether a contract came into existence at all, and then which terms govern the contract. See further Section 6.3.

4.6   At What Point Was the Acceptance Made?

Once having decided that a valid and unqualified acceptance has been made, it is important to determine when the acceptance becomes operative, because from that time the contract is binding on both parties. The normal rule is that the acceptance is valid from the time it is communicated to the offeror. Communication involves notice having been brought to the attention of the offeror, whether it has actually been assimilated by reading the acceptance letter or not. It has been held that something positive must be done in order to effect an acceptance: e.g. in the case of Mrs Carlill it was sniffing the smoke ball. Express communication is not always necessary if it is implied in the offer that performance is sufficient. However, doing nothing at all cannot be a valid acceptance as shown in the case of *Felthouse* v *Bindley* [1862] 11 CBNS 869 where the statement 'if I hear no more about him I consider the horse is mine' was insufficient as a valid acceptance. (This rule could have been of use to the victims of inertia-selling techniques if they had known about it – see Section 9.7).

An exception to the rule requiring communication of acceptance is the so-called 'Postal Rule'. This developed in the nineteenth century to deal with problems of delays in communication due to the use of the postal service (which actually often delivered letters very quickly at that time – letters written in the morning could arrive by the afternoon post!). Therefore communication was not instantaneous as in face-to-face negotiations. In such cases as *Henthorn* v *Fraser* [1892] 2 Ch. 27 it was held that the acceptance was valid from the time the letter of acceptance was posted, regardless of when or if it arrived, provided it was properly stamped, addressed and posted, and that the post was the expected method of communication. This had implications with regard to the rules about revoking or cancelling an offer, for there it was decided that a revocation was only valid when it arrived. Thus an offeror could make an offer by post on a Monday, which was accepted by a letter posted on Tuesday but not arriving until Friday. Meanwhile the offeror having changed his or her mind had written on Wednesday to cancel the offer, that is before receiving the acceptance, this letter arriving on Thursday. However, because the offer had been technically accepted on Tuesday the revocation was invalid, even though the offeree knew of this before the offeror knew of the acceptance! This rule has also been applied to other more modern non-instantaneous methods of communication such as cables and telegrams, but not to instantaneous ones such as telex and telephones.

However, some doubt has been thrown on the application of this rule to telexes. In the recent decision of *Brinkibon Ltd.* v *Stahag Stahl* [1983] A.C. 34 it was pointed out that sometimes telexes are not instantaneous as the message may be received outside working hours at night or during the weekend. In the case in hand, this was held not to apply and the contract was made when it was communicated via telex to Vienna, and therefore another case involving telexes is required before the position can be stated with any certainty.

Obviously it can cause problems for businesses to be held to be bound by an offer they have made before they are aware it has been accepted. It is possible to override the application of the postal rule by making it a condition of the offer that acceptance is not valid until it is received. In the case of *Holwell Securities Ltd.* v *Hughes* [1974] 1 All E.R. 161, this was achieved by simply stating that notice in writing was required. It is also possible to lay down in the offer the method of acceptance that is required, and if this is not complied with no contract will be made.

The place where acceptance is made may also be important as it may govern which law regulates the contract. In the *Brinkibon* case above, it was held to be subject to Austrian Law because acceptance occurred in Vienna. However, to avoid this happening it can be clearly stated in the offer that English Law governs the contract.

4.7 Was There an Element of Consideration in the Agreement?

The requirement for consideration in a contract is because the English courts are not prepared to enforce a one-sided gratuitous promise, but must see evidence of an exchange of promises, or a bargain, having been struck. In business situations, this usually causes few problems as the exchange of promises comprises goods or services in return for payment.

Consideration need not be in the form of money, although it is often referred to as 'the price paid for a promise'. It may be something else of value to the other party, such as providing professional services in return for goods, or exchanging one type of goods for another.

Several aspects of the rules regarding consideration may be of importance in a commercial context, however, and they will be looked at in turn.

(a) Consideration must have some value
Although the courts want to see the parties exchange or promise to exchange something of value they are not concerned with the worth of the consideration. The parties can enter into whatever agreement they choose provided there is no duress or fraud involved. So a contract cannot be challenged on the basis that the consideration provided is too small or too large: for example, that the agreed price for goods was far too low or too high in relation to what was provided in return. If a business chooses to sell fur coats or Rolls Royces at £5 each, or holiday companies sell bargain holidays, this does not affect the validity of the contract, which will be binding.

A point that sometimes causes confusion is to assume that if one party never provides the consideration, for example refuses to pay the agreed price, then there is no contract due to an absence of the essential element of consideration. This is not so. The fact that the promise is broken or never fulfilled means that the contract is broken, not that it has never been made.

(b) Past consideration
In order to be recognised as a valuable consideration, the promise must be given in return for the other and not given after the promise has been made or some gratuitous service carried out. This is known as past consideration and is illustrated by *Roscorla* v *Thomas* [1842] 3 Q.B. 234 where negotiations for the sale of a horse had been concluded. The seller then promised that the horse was 'sound and free from vice', which turned out to be untrue. However, the buyer could not sue for the breach of this promise because no consideration had been provided in return for it. The price had been paid for the promised transfer of ownership of the horse so that consideration was past at the time of the new promise. This may be an important factor if negotiations continue after the agreement has been made, as promises made after this time will

not be binding due to an absence of consideration. This means that terms written on pieces of paper sent after the contract has been made, such as confirmation notes or invoices, will not be part of the contract, unless these terms have been settled beforehand and simply confirmed in writing, or are implied into the agreement as a result of previous dealings between the parties. See further Section 6.2.

(c) A promise to do no more than is already required to be done will be no consideration

As consideration must have some value, a party that merely promises to do no more than is already required of him by virtue of his employment, public duty or previous contract, cannot be regarded as consideration for another promise. This can be particularly relevant in the case of an agreement to allow another person to pay less than previously agreed to discharge a debt. In *D. & C. Builders* v *Rees* [1966] 2 Q.B. 617, Mrs Rees persuaded the builders to accept £300 in full and final settlement of a debt of £482. However, the firm was able to recover the remainder of the amount at a later date because Mrs Rees had provided nothing in return for their promise to accept the lower sum; she had only done part of what she was already obliged to do! However, if she had made payment in a different form, or perhaps earlier than she was obliged to do so, this would have been good consideration for D & C's promise.

(d) Consideration must pass from the promisee

Only the party who provides consideration will be able to sue on the promise, so no-one on behalf of whom a contract is made can sue under the contract if he himself has not provided consideration, unless the promisee was acting as his agent (see Chapter 7). This rule is also known as privity of contract and its importance will be clear at a later stage, see Sections 5.12 and 10.2.

(e) 'Free' gifts

What is the position with goods or services that are offered as 'free'? Can a contract be said to exist in these circumstances, if, as would appear, no consideration is required from the recipient of the gift? The answer is not absolutely clear. There is a possibility that the court would hold no contract exists because there was no intention to create legal relations, as was argued unsuccessfully in the case of *Esso Petroleum Ltd.* v *Customs & Excise Commissioners*

[1976] 1 All E.R. 117, which involved the supply of free World Cup coins. However, if this point is overcome it would normally be possible to argue that the consideration provided by the recipient is the requirement to enter into another contract in order to obtain the free gift: for example in the *Esso* case the requirement to buy four gallons of petrol. This would therefore be regarded as a collateral or subsidiary contract.

It may be asked why it would be necessary to prove the existence of a contract in the case of free goods and it is highly unlikely that anyone would feel sufficiently moved to sue for the right to obtain plastic World Cup coins and such like. However, often much more substantial goods, such as electrical equipment, may be offered free as part of a sales promotion, and then it may be necessary to prove a contract existed in order to take advantage of the implied terms which are present in contracts. See further Section 5.3.

4.8   Capacity to Contract

Apart from satisfying themselves that the essential elements of a contract as outlined above are present, the courts will also want to be sure that the parties concluding an agreement have the capacity, or legal ability, to make it binding. Some individuals, for their own protection, do not have full capacity, that is minors under the age of 18 and mentally ill people. Artificial persons, that is companies, (see Section 3.5) are also limited in what they can do.

In England and Wales, minors can only be bound by contracts that they enter into for 'necessaries', or contracts which are on the whole of benefit to them. Necessaries are defined by reference to the needs of the particular minor concerned, and therefore when supplying goods to minors it is as well to insist on cash sales only. Any request for payment later or fulfilment of credit obligations may be met with the response that the contract is unenforceable as it is not for necessaries. It is not entirely clear whether the requirement of an adult guarantor would protect a seller in these circumstances, as this contract also may be unenforceable. Contracts of employment for young people should be enforceable unless the terms are such that the young person has obviously been exploited because of his or her inexperience and the terms are onerous. Similar rules concerning necessaries apply to those suffering from a mental illness.

Any contract entered into during a period of drunkenness (perhaps during an over-indulgent business lunch or conference) is voidable. It can be made void by action taken as soon as sobriety returns. This is so, however, only if it was or should have been obvious to the other party that the would-be contractor was affected by drink.

The main restriction on a company's capacity is to be found in the objects clause of its memorandum of association (see Section 3.5). This lays down what the company has been set up to do and is open to public inspection. Any contract entered into which is *ultra vires* this clause will be void, even if the shareholders have 'authorised' the deal. This was decided in *Ashbury Railway Carriage & Iron Co.* v *Riche* [1875] L.R. 7 H.L. 653 when a company which had been set up to build railway carriages entered into a contract to lay railway lines in Belgium. All the contracts were unenforceable, even though they had been approved by the shareholders in a general meeting.

The harshness of this rule, which would require a constant check to be kept on the memoranda of association of each company with which a business dealt, has been tempered by two factors, one legal and one practical. The practical point is that objects clauses nowadays are drawn up very widely indeed to cover most possible developments that the company would like to move into. It is also possible, of course, to amend the objects clause in the way authorised by the Companies Act 1985 if need be.

The legal move was initiated by UK membership of the European Community and was necessary to bring us into line with the practice in other EEC countries. The provision is now found in the Companies Act 1985, s. 35. It states that where another person enters into a contract agreed by the directors in good faith, then such a contract will be binding against the company, regardless of whether it is *intra vires*. The company acting *ultra vires*, however, would still not be able to enforce the contract. The exact scope of this rule is not entirely clear as it is not yet certain how strictly 'agreed upon by the directors' will be interpreted. However, it does provide some protection for those who deal with companies.

4.9 Mistakes in the Contract

The general rule regarding mistakes in relation to contracts is that they will not affect their validity, unless they strike at a fundamental aspect of the agreement, and it can therefore be argued that agreement was never reached and no contract existed at all.

Examples of such fundamental misunderstandings would be where the parties are talking about two entirely different things, or where the subject matter of the contract unknown to either party no longer exists at the time the contract is made. But mistakes as to the value of the subject matter, such as in *Leaf* v *International Galleries* [1950] 2 K.B. 86 where both parties thought they were dealing with a Constable painting when in fact it was of lesser worth, will not nullify the contract. The disappointed buyer may, however, have a remedy for *misrepresentation*.

In cases where the mistakes arise from wrong information being included in written documents after oral agreement, the courts will generally allow these to be rectified if sufficient evidence can be produced to substantiate the claim.

4.10   Ending a Contract

A contract normally ends automatically when both parties have carried out their parts of the bargain to their mutual satisfaction. Sometimes, however, the parties will agree to bring the contract to an end before full performance is completed. This will be binding on both if both are giving something in return, i.e. each is providing consideration for that of the other. However if one party has performed his or her side of the bargain completely but the other has not, a promise to allow this will only be binding if there is some consideration for it. See Section 4.7*(c)* above.

Occasionally contracts will end because they are impossible to carry out, for example because of an unforeseeable change in circumstances, such as new government regulations or war breaking out between the respective companies' countries. The courts are only prepared to allow such circumstances to end a contract in very extreme cases, when they apply what is known as the doctrine of frustration. However, where contracts are simply made commercially very difficult then this doctrine will not apply. For example when the Suez Canal was closed in the 1950s, contracts which were broken as a result of this were held not to have been frustrated and damages had to be paid. In order to avoid this restrictive interpretation many businesses include *force majeure* clauses in their standard terms, particularly when dealing with foreign companies, which lay down the circumstances in which the parties agree that the contract should end. See further Section 6.5.

When a contract is broken (or 'breached') by one or other party, then depending on the importance of the term that has been broken, this may result in the contract ending. Terms of contracts are divided into two major groups, conditions or warranties. When a condition, or fundamentally important term, is broken, the contract automatically ends, which releases the other party from any obligations under the contract and gives him the right to sue for damages. On the other hand, if the term is considered a warranty, or less important term, then such a breach only gives the right to sue for damages while the contract continues to operate. The difficulty arises in deciding whether a term is a condition or warranty. Sometimes this does not become clear until the breach occurs and the importance of the term can then be judged. For these purposes, it does not matter what the two parties have called the term as ultimately it is for the courts to decide.

4.11   Remedies for Breach of Contract

(a) Damages
As has already been noted, the main remedy for breach of contract is damages. Damages are primarily a means of compensating for loss suffered and are not intended as a punishment of the other party. Therefore it is highly unlikely that a profit will be made from a claim for damages, except in exceptional cases where exemplary or punitive damages are awarded.

The amount, or *quantum*, of damages that can be claimed is therefore primarily calculated by assessing how much monetary loss has been suffered as a direct consequence of the breach of contract. This will include damage to plant and equipment, any personal injuries and loss of profits (economic loss). However, it is by no means certain that the total amount will be recovered because of the application of the following rules in calculating damages.

In *Hadley* v *Baxendale* [1854] 9 Exch 341, loss was occasioned as a result of the late delivery of the crankshaft of a mill. It was held that damages could be awarded under two headings; firstly, those which were the natural consequences arising from such a breach, and secondly those which were a result of any special circumstances which were known or should have been known to the parties when the contract was made. On this basis, the mill owner did not recover his entire loss, as certain consequences were not within the knowledge of the repairer at the time. It therefore follows that it is essential to inform the other party to a contract of any unusual or particularly costly plans which depend on the performance of the contract, for example an export order or major dealership arrangement, in order to be able to claim for that loss if need be.

Where a contract provides for the supply of goods or services which are easily obtainable elsewhere, the measure of damages for non-delivery or non-acceptance of the product would be the difference between the contract price and the market price at the time of breach. Should there be no difference in price then no damage has been suffered and substantial damages cannot be claimed except perhaps nominal damages of £1 or so to 'mark the breach'. In such circumstances, it is obviously not worth the time or trouble to assert one's legal rights against the party in breach. But when goods or services are of a specialised nature, and not readily available elsewhere, the damages may be the entire loss on the deal. However, there is a duty on the party claiming damages to mitigate his loss by making reasonable efforts to minimise the damage suffered. It is not possible to sit back thinking to recover all losses from the party in breach, for the courts will consider by how much damage could have been mitigated and reduce the award by that amount.

To avoid the difficulties inherent in the calculation of damages many businesses include 'liquidated damages' clauses in their contracts. Such a clause would specify the amount to be paid in the event of an anticipated breach, and provided this is a genuine pre-estimate of expected loss and not a penalty designed to terrify the other party into performing the contract correctly it will be enforceable. See further Section 6.6.

(b) Specific performance

When it is said that the courts will enforce the contract, it often suggests that they will force the party to carry it out. However, such an order is very rarely granted, because it is so difficult for the court to ensure that it is done, and anyway a reluctant contracting party will rarely perform the task well. It is generally considered therefore that money damages are sufficient compensation for the breach, and a sufficient incentive to ensure that most contracts are kept when this is coupled with consideration of business reputation and expediency. In certain rare cases, however, a decree of specific performance will be granted to order the contract to be carried out. This is when the subject matter of the contract is unique, and money compensation would not be sufficient. It has most application in contracts concerning the sale of land, but it might also apply to agreements for the sale of unique antiques or shares in a private company. In most other situations, damages must suffice.

(c) Injunctions

The courts are reluctant to grant injunctions in cases involving breach of contract because such an order would require some supervision by the court to ensure it was obeyed. An injunction may be occasionally granted to prevent someone from breaking a contractual obligation, usually in a contract of employment, such as that they will not join a rival business for, say, three years after leaving their current employment. Here money would be an empty compensation once the employee had already joined the rival and probably disclosed details of the previous employer's operations. The courts would have to be satisfied that the restriction on individual freedom was reasonable. See further Section 12.3.

Both injunctions and specific performance are discretionary orders and will not automatically be granted, as damages would be once a case is made out. Two particular types of injunctions may be of use in the course of a case involving breach of contract.

Mareva Injunctions, named after the case in which such an order was first granted, allow a plaintiff to stop the defendants from removing assets from the jurisdiction before a full hearing of the case. Such an order would be useful against a foreign business, because if all the assets were removed then there would be no way in which a successful plaintiff could recover judgement. Very often, even when judgement is obtained against another business, particularly a small business, it may be necessary to take further action against its assets to recover any damages that have been awarded as this is not done automatically by the courts.

Anton Piller Injunctions are also useful in order to obtain possession of documents or other matters that are in the hands of an agent in order to prevent them from being disclosed in breach of the agent's duty of good faith. However, these are only rarely granted and would be very strictly supervised by a solicitor or other party appointed by the court.

Questions

1   What are the three basic requirements of an agreement which is legally enforceable, i.e. a contract?

2   Explain briefly the facts and decisions in the following cases, and state what their importance is for businesses.

> *Hadley* v *Baxendale*
> *British Road Services* v *Arthur Crutchley*
> *British Steel Corporation* v *Cleveland Bridge & Engineering Co. Ltd.*
> *Carlill* v *The Carbolic Smoke Ball Company.*

If a Law Library is available near you then read these cases in full. It will give you a better understanding of each case and of how the courts work in general.

3   Why do businesses often buy an option when an offer is made to them to buy goods in the future?

4   What is the postal rule?

5   What are meant by the phrases

(a)   past consideration
(b)   liquidated damages
(c)   necessaries?

6   What is the difference between a condition and a warranty?

7   When would a Mareva Injunction be useful?

Before attempting questions 8, 9 and 10 please read the section at the end of the book on answering problem questions.

8   On 12 June J. Smith & Sons Ltd., a supplier of fancy goods sent out a circular headed SPECIAL OFFER TO OUR PRIZED CUSTOMERS! LOW, LOW PRICES!

> 200 Halloween masks at £2.00 each.
> 5000 Stink Bombs at £1.00 per hundred.
> 300 Boxes Crazy Foam at £4.00 each.
> 600 EZ size boxed fireworks at £3.00 each.

Crazy Crafts Limited received a copy of this circular on 15 June and wrote back immediately ordering 100 Halloween masks and 500 Stink Bombs. This letter arrived on J. Smith's desk on 16 June.

Meanwhile, on Saturday morning Mr Green who had received his circular that morning, walked around to J. Smith's premises and posted through their door an order for all 200 Halloween masks. On Monday morning, on opening this, J. Smith sent out a further circular, withdrawing the Halloween masks from sale. Crazy Crafts received this on Wednesday, 17 June.

Advise Crazy Crafts on whether they have a binding contract for 100 Halloween masks at £2.00 each.

9   A. Limited sends a cable to a company in France, B., offering to sell a piece of machinery to them for £5000. The French company replied by placing an order for the machinery and stating that they will pay in French Francs. A. Limited failed to deliver the machinery. Advise B.

10   Advise C. Company as to the remedy available to them, if any, in the following situations:

   (a) Their bid for £15 000 for an oil painting by an Old Master to be hung in the boardroom is accepted at an auction, but the seller changes her mind and refuses to deliver the painting.

   (b) D. Company failed to supply some component parts for use in the manufacturing process. After some delay, replacements are found at a slightly lower price.

   (c) E. Company supplied deficient materials for use in the manufacturing process. As a result of this delay a major contract with an American company is lost.

   (d) A clause in their contract with a building company F. for re-fitting an office provides for payment of £50 each week that F. is behind schedule. The office is six weeks late in completion.

Chapter 5
The Sale of Goods Act 1979 and The Supply of Goods and Services Act 1982

In addition to the Common Law rules which constitute the law of contract dealt with in the previous chapter, there are additional laws in statutory form which apply to specific types of contract. It is important to bear in mind that these are supplementary to and not separate from the law in Chapter 4.

The two pieces of legislation referred to in the title of this Chapter have been passed by Parliament in an attempt to clarify the rights and responsibilities of the parties to specific types of contract if they themselves have not dealt with the matter. The Acts do not attempt to lay down what should or should not be in the contract, but simply apply if the contract itself is silent on the point. With the exception of the implied terms (see Sections 5.3 and 5.4) everything dealt with by the Acts can be varied or excluded by agreement of the parties. As the original draftsman of the Sale of Goods Act said:

> 'Sale is a consensual contract, and the Act does not seek to prevent the parties from making any bargain they please. Its object is to lay down clear rules for the case where the parties have either formed no intention, or failed to express it'.
>
> Sir Mackenzie Chalmer.

This legislation is therefore useful as a back-up but in most commercial contracts, especially those using carefully drafted standard terms and conditions, it will not be necessary to refer to it at all, as the questions will have been dealt with in the contract.

The following chapter will outline the main provisions of these Acts and point out when they may be important.

5.1 The Background to the Sale of Goods Act 1979

As has been shown, the law of contract was built up over the decades through decisions of the courts, but the sheer number of cases meant that inevitably there was overlapping of subject areas and occasional contradictory decisions. As a result, in 1893 Parliament took on the task of codifying the law in the most heavily litigated area, namely involving contracts for the sale of goods, into a statute to clarify the position and make the job of lawyers and commercial people easier when looking for the law. This Act, the Sale of Goods Act, was thus based on existing precedents and was not an attempt to introduce new laws. In 1979, after several amendments had been made to the Act, the statute was consolidated, which means that it was reintroduced largely in the same form but incorporating all the amendments. This history of the Act helps to explain why what sounds like a new piece of legislation is in fact rather full of anachronistic terms such as 'merchantable quality' and outdated concepts such as 'market overt' (see below). The legislation is therefore not ideal for dealing with modern commercial situations and this provides another incentive for businesses to ensure that the contracts they negotiate, either individually or in standard form, clearly reflect all their intentions, so that the legislation need not come into play.

5.2 When Does the Sale of Goods Act Apply?

It is to be emphasised that the parties to a contract for a sale of goods are in no way bound to take the Act into account when making a contract. In order for such a contract to be valid it must comply with the rules laid out in Chapter 4. The parties can come to whatever agreement they choose and it is only if they forget to include a point, or overlook its importance during negotiations, which subsequently appears to be important during the course of the performance of the contract, that the Sale of Goods Act can be referred to to determine the position of the parties.

As its name implies, the Sale of Goods Act applies only to contracts for the sale of goods, defined in section 2 as contracts by which the seller transfers or agrees to transfer property in goods to the buyer for a money consideration called the price. The property in the goods means the right of ownership. Thus the Act is confined to cash sales of goods.

'Goods' include such items as crops and animals as well as other forms of personal property, but does not include money (unless for instance rare coins are bought and sold) or property referred to as 'choses in action' which means personal property of an intangible nature like debts, copyright and shares. Also not covered by the Act are goods bought as part of a package including services as well, e.g. when radiators and a boiler are sold as part of a contract to install central heating in a house or a factory, as such contracts are regarded as contracts for work and materials. Neither are hire-purchase or hiring contracts covered, nor contracts where goods are exchanged for trading stamps or other vouchers or other goods, unless some money changes hands in part-exchange. Over time other legislation has had to be introduced to deal with some aspects of these types of contract in a piecemeal fashion, for example see the Consumer Credit Act, Section 11.5, and the Supply of Goods and Services Act, below.

The first ten sections of the Act, apart from defining what is meant by a contract of sale, broadly restate the general principles of contract law, so that section 8 for example deals with the matter of price by confirming that the price is that agreed by the parties, or agreed to be determined by the parties in a fixed manner, or failing this, should be reasonable.

5.3   The Implied Terms

Sections 12–15 of the Sale of Goods Act make it clear that certain terms are part of each contract of sale regardless of whether the parties have agreed to them or not. These implied terms are in contrast to the express terms as to price, delivery dates, etc. on which the parties have negotiated and agreed explicitly. Originally, as with all other provisions of the Sale of Goods Act, these terms could be excluded by express agreement between the parties and this was done almost as a matter of course in most business transactions. However, the ability to do this is now limited by the Unfair Contract Terms Act. See Section 5.4 and Section 6.4 below.

(a) Section 12 makes it a condition of the contract that the seller has the right to sell the goods and can transfer a good title, another term meaning rights of ownership, to the buyer. The effect of this is that if for some reason the seller has not got the title, for example because the goods were stolen, then the buyer may claim a lawful refund of the price and damages as a condition of the contract has been broken, provided only of course that the seller can be traced!

(b) **Section 13** states that it is a condition of the contract that where goods are sold by description they must correspond with this description. The mere fact that the goods have been chosen or selected by the buyer does not mean there has not been a sale by description. Thus where a car was sold having been described in an advertisement as a Herald Convertible 1961 but after being inspected by the buyer, it was held that section 13 had been breached when it turned out that only half of it matched its description, the other half being part of another model which had been welded to the front: *Beale* v *Taylor* [1967] 3 All E.R. 258. This term has very often been strictly interpreted by the courts and buyers have been able to reject whole consignments because, for example, tins were packed in cartons of 25 instead of 30 as ordered, or because 1 cm thick planks were in fact 1.2 cm thick, although very minor deviations will be ignored.

(c) **Section 14** applies only where goods are sold in the course of a business and not to private sellers. It should be noted that the other implied terms do not have this qualification, and therefore apply equally to private sellers.

It is first made clear that the old maxim *caveat emptor,* let the buyer beware, is to remain except as modified by the section. Thus no other terms as to quality, fitness or usefulness of the goods can be implied, and it would be for the buyer to ensure that any other required standards were expressly agreed upon in the course of the contract. The implied terms are:

(i) The goods must be of merchantable quality (subsection 2). This is defined in subsection 6 and broadly means that the goods must be reasonably fit for their normal purpose, bearing in mind their description and price. This is not the case if the defects are pointed out to the buyer, or the buyer has inspected the goods and should have noticed the defects. Note that there is no requirement for the buyer to inspect the goods. What is reasonably fit is a question of fact to be determined in each case, but minor defects that can fairly easily be put right are unlikely to render goods unmerchantable.

(ii) The goods must be reasonably fit for the particular purpose made known by the buyer, expressly or by implication, whether or not this is the normal purpose of the goods (subsection 3). This does not apply if the buyer did not rely on the seller's judgement, or it was unreasonable for the buyer so to do.

It is immediately apparent that subsections 2 and 3 overlap to a large extent, and indeed most buyers would rely on both if rejecting goods based on a defect. The reason for the overlap is that before 1973 'merchantable' quality had not been defined and was left to the courts to determine. When a definition was included in the Act it was close to the existing requirements for goods to be fit for their purpose. The difference between them is primarily that only subsection 3 would be applicable if goods were bought to be used for a purpose other than the normal one, provided this had been made clear before the contract was made, or if clear specifications had been given. It is therefore essential for buyers to give as much information as possible to the seller about the purpose for which goods are required. This enables them later to reject the goods if they do not fulfil these requirements on the basis of subsection 3.

(d) **Section 15** requires that goods bought in reliance on a sample should match that sample in quality when the bulk is delivered. Again this is an implied condition, and breach allows the purchaser to reject the goods, demand repayment of the purchase price already paid and compensation for any consequential damage suffered.

These terms therefore give buyers some protection as to the goods they are purchasing, provided they were not effectively excluded from the contract.

5.4 Exclusion of the Implied Terms

Since 1973 the right to contract out of the implied terms has been subject to statutory regulation and the law is now found in the Unfair Contract Terms Act 1977. This Act will be dealt with in more detail later (see Section 6.4) but in the present context it prohibits the exclusion of section 12 from any contract, i.e. this term is present in every contract for the sale of goods. Exclusion of the other terms is possible, but only in contracts between businesses and only if the term meets the requirement of 'reasonableness'. See Section 6.4 for the details of this requirement. A contract of sale made between a business and a consumer will always include the implied terms in sections 13–15, and it is a criminal offence to purport to exclude them. For the purposes of this legislation, a consumer is defined as a person who neither acts in the course of a business nor holds themselves out as doing so, who deals with another person acting in the course of a business, and who buys goods of the kind ordinarily supplied for private use.

It is therefore still common for businesses to include clauses in their contracts with other businesses which state that the implied terms do not form part of their contracts. Whether such a clause is effective will depend on the reasonableness test, but as this is so uncertain and really needs testing in court each time to determine the clause's validity it is unlikely that commercial organisations will drop this practice. Even if such a clause would be declared to be unreasonable, the chances of its being tested in court are minimal due to the reasons given in Section 2.4 and so such clauses continue to be successfully used and relied upon. However, it is as well to ensure that the clauses are not clearly unreasonable, to minimise the risk of them being challenged.

5.5   Transfer of Ownership and Risk

Sections 16–19 of the Sale of Goods Act lay down rules for determining at what point the rights of ownership pass from the seller to the buyer. This will be important to know in two situations:

(a) if the buyer goes into liquidation before paying for the goods, the sellers will want to know if the goods are still technically owned by them and so can be recovered without waiting to be paid as unsecured creditors, and

(b) if the goods are destroyed through neither party's fault the loss will have to be borne by the owner of goods at that point.

Very often these aspects will be clearly dealt with in the contract by the use of Romalpa clauses (see Section 6.7) and a statement as to when the risk passes from one to another, but if it is not then the Sale of Goods Act rules apply.

This part of the Act makes a distinction between unascertained goods and specific (or ascertained) goods. The former are not defined in the Statute but can be understood in contrast to the latter, which are defined as goods which are identified and agreed upon at the time a contract of sale is made. Hence the goods must be in existence and identifiable at the time agreement is reached. Unascertained goods therefore may be part of a mass of goods at present stored elsewhere, perhaps in a warehouse, or may yet to be manufactured at the time of the contract. The distinction is important because section 16 states that property in the goods cannot be transferred until unascertained goods are ascertained,

therefore before they are manufactured to the buyer's specifications or in some way conclusively set aside as forming the
subject matter of the contract they will remain the property of the
seller.

Once goods are ascertained, or if the contract is for specific
goods, section 17 states that property in them is transferred when
the parties intended it to be, such intention to be gleaned from the
contract itself or other conduct of the parties. But should this be
impossible to discover, section 18 helpfully gives five rules for
determining the parties' intention.

Rule 1 says that when specific goods in a deliverable state (i.e. to
which nothing further need be done), are sold, property passes to
the buyer when the contract is made, regardless of the time of
payment or delivery. However, the courts might be willing to infer
from the circumstances that property was not to pass until either or
both of these have occurred. But as the goods are the buyer's, the
buyer must arrange insurance cover from that point. This is
another reason why it is important to be able to determine at which
point the contract is made. (See Section 4.6.)

Rule 2 allows for specific goods being put into a deliverable state,
when property will pass only when this has been done and the
buyer is informed.

Rule 3 allows for the situation where the seller has to weigh or
measure the goods to determine the price, and again property does
not pass until this is done and the buyer is informed.

Rule 4 relates to goods supplied on sale or return, and property
does not pass until the buyer signifies that the goods are to be
retained or returned, or if this is not done, within a reasonable
time.

Rule 5 is the only one which deals with unascertained goods,
although the majority of commercial contracts of any size are likely
to be for unascertained or future goods because they will not yet
have been manufactured. This rule states that the property passes
when goods are 'unconditionally appropriated' to the contract with
the express or implied assent of the buyer and seller. Good
evidence for such appropriation would be when the seller consigns
the goods to a carrier, or delivers them into the possession of the
buyer, but it may occur at an earlier stage when the goods are set to
one side for the buyer and clearly identified by labelling or
otherwise as being the subject matter of the contract.

It is obviously essential to the buyer to be fully insured from the point where the transfer of property occurs, as section 20 makes it clear that risk of loss is transferred with property, unless the contrary is agreed, even though this may be some time before the goods are under the control or in the possession of the buyer.

Section 19 states that ownership may be retained by the seller until some condition is met. Recently it has become common for sellers to require that the condition is that the full price is paid. How successful these attempts have been will be considered when Romalpa clauses are examined later (see Section 6.7).

5.6   The *Nemo Dat* Rule

The full name of this rule is *nemo dat quod non habet* and it means that no-one can pass on a better title to goods than that which he or she possesses. This is stated in section 21 of the Sale of Goods Act. Thus the buyer of stolen goods has no better right to the goods than the seller, that is none, and if traced the goods can be returned to the original owner who will still retain ownership rights.

However, there are a number of exceptions to this rule, which protect innocent purchasers in circumstances where they had no reason to assume there was anything wrong with the title of the goods. There are six main ways laid down in sections 21–25 of the Act in which the buyer will get good title, leaving the true owner to take action against the seller.

(a) The true owner of the goods has made it appear that the seller has the right to sell.
(b) Where a mercantile agent has the goods in his or her possession to sell but sells against the owner's instructions, e.g. at a lower price. A mercantile agent is one who customarily sells goods on behalf of their owners.
(c) When goods are sold in market overt. This means in an established marketplace, or in shops in the City of London, and in accordance with the normal rules of the market. The sale must also take place between sunrise and sunset, a leftover from the days before electric lights made this factor an irrelevance!
(d) Where the seller has a voidable title to the goods, but this has not been avoided at the time of the sale. This might be where, for instance, the goods were sold originally relying on a misrepresentation and would not have been sold if the true facts were known. However, if this had not yet been discovered, the original

sale was still valid and therefore the second buyer would receive a good title.

(e) Where the seller has already sold the goods to someone else but continues to possess them and re-sells them to a second bona fide purchaser.

(f) Where the seller has bought the goods from someone else but has yet to have title passed to him or her by the original seller. This may happen where for example, the original seller included a condition on transfer of title which exists after delivery.

In all these circumstances buyers would have to show that they bought in good faith, i.e. without any notice of the sellers' lack of title in order to be protected and become the new owners of the goods.

5.7   Performance of the Contract

Part IV of the Sale of Goods Act deals with matters affecting the performance of the contract, that is the delivery and acceptance of the goods. Section 27 states that it is the duty of the seller of goods to deliver the goods and the buyer to accept and pay for them in accordance with the terms of the contract. Delivery does not require the seller to physically transfer the goods in the normal commercial sense of the word, but simply to allow the buyer to take possession of the goods in whatever way is agreed between the parties. Again if this is not agreed between the parties, the Act gives the answer.

Section 29 lays down that it is for the buyer to collect the goods from the seller unless otherwise agreed. Where goods are delivered in instalments a question often arises if one instalment is late or defective in some way. Does this mean that the whole contract can be rejected and delivery of any future instalments not taken? The answer depends on whether the contract is severable or non-severable, i.e. can it be considered to be a series of contracts or just one complete contract performed in part? This the court will determine by looking at the terms of the contract and the circumstances of the case. One general point can be made however. The question of late delivery may be regarded as breach of a condition of the contract. Generally, unless the contrary is expressed, 'time is of the essence' of a commercial contract: i.e. the time at which the contract is to be performed is usually a vital term, or condition of the contract. Therefore breach of that term would give rise to the right to reject the goods, reclaim the money paid and claim damages. Often businesses are not going to want to make use of this right, as what they want is the goods, on time if at all possible, and so to try to ensure this, liquidated damages clauses are often relied on rather than the strict legal right of repudiating the contract. See Section 4.11*(a)* and 6.6.

The question of *when* the buyer is deemed to have accepted the goods is also important because once having done so, the right to reject the goods is lost, although a right to claim damages is retained. Sections 34 and 35 lay down that the buyer has accepted the goods when the seller has been told so expressly, or when the buyer does something to them which indicates that they are considered as being accepted, for example, using materials in a manufacturing process, or after the lapse of a reasonable amount of time. This is subject to the right of a buyer who has not previously examined the goods, not to be deemed to have accepted the goods until there has been a reasonable opportunity for inspecting them.

This part of the Act also states, among other things, that it is for the seller to retrieve rejected goods from the buyer, and makes the buyer liable to compensate the seller for unreasonable refusal to take delivery of the goods when this is proffered by the seller.

5.8   Remedies under the Sale of Goods Act

Part V of the Sale of Goods Act gives a series of rights to the seller over the goods, even once property in them has been transferred, until payment is made. For instance the seller has a limited right known as a *lien* to retain possession of the goods or to stop them in transit if the buyer becomes insolvent after the seller has parted with the goods.

Part VI deals with actions for breach of contract and basically restates the general principles of contract law, i.e. that damages are payable for non-acceptance by the buyer or non-delivery by the seller, and the measure of damages is the difference between the agreed price and the market price at the time of the breach where there is an available market for the goods in question.

For further details of these and other matters dealt with here the Act itself should be consulted when such points have not been included in the contract itself. It is of course advisable for all these matters to be decided upon in advance and included in the express terms of the contract so as to avoid conflict and delay during or after performance of the contract.

5.9   The Background to the Supply of Goods and Services Act

The 1982 Act was passed as the result of pressure by consumer groups to clarify the law in relation to contracts of services, and where goods were supplied other than by a contract of sale. The business community appeared to be very concerned on its introduction although in reality the Act does not impose many new obligations on businesses.

The Act covers contracts for the supply of goods which are not contracts of sale, hire-purchase, or involve the transfer of trading stamps, and therefore includes so-called free gifts, contracts of exchange and barter, contracts for work and materials or service contracts, and contracts of hire and leasing. However, it is nowhere near as comprehensive in coverage as the Sale of Goods Act and deals solely with implied terms in these contracts, and not with all the other matters that have been dealt with above in relation to the 1979 Act.

5.10   Part I of the Supply of Goods and Services Act

Part I of the Act deals with contracts for the supply of goods and broadly states that in contracts of this type all the implied terms that are found in the Sale of Goods Act sections 12–15, as set out in Section 5.3 above, are also to be implied into every contract for the supply of goods. The only modification is for contracts of hire, where there is obviously no implied term of the right to transfer ownership, but the right to non-interference during the period of hire is guaranteed instead.

The effect of this Act is to ensure that whenever goods are supplied under whatever type of contract is involved, the same implied terms will be in them. (Contracts where trading stamps or hire-purchase are involved also include these terms by virtue of their own, specialised legislation). So the customers' rights, be they businesses or consumers, do not depend on a technicality as to what type of contract may have been made. In the case of a consumer sale, these terms can never be excluded, and in a business-to-business sale the terms can only be excluded if the exclusion clause meets the requirement of reasonableness (see Section 6.4).

As these are implied conditions in the contract, breach would allow the contract to be ended and a claim for damages to be made.

5.11   Part II of the Supply of Goods and Services Act

Part II of the Act is concerned with contracts of services by which the supplier undertakes to carry out a service of some kind in the course of a business, such as building work or professional services. The contract may of course include the supply of goods as well, in which case Part I would apply to it in addition to Part II.

Part II requires that all such contracts should be carried out with reasonable care and skill, within a reasonable time if none is set and at a reasonable price if none has been agreed. Whether or not such terms could be excluded would depend on the provisions of the Unfair Contract Terms Act (see Section 6.4). What is reasonable depends on all the circumstances of the case and is a matter of fact, but professionals would be judged by the standards of professional people, and not by their own standards or those of unqualified people. It is unlikely that this part of the Act imposes any higher obligation than previously existed under the Common Law.

5.12   Situations Outside the Scope of the Legislation

A final point that should be emphasised about these Acts is that they relate only to contracts of sale or supply, and therefore because of the privity of contract rule (see Section 4.7(*d*)) only the parties to the contract can rely on these provisions. This may be important when sub-contractors fulfil part of the obligations under a primary contract between A & B. There will be no liability in contract between A and the sub-contractors, who were hired by B. A more difficult claim for negligence might have to be taken if for some reason it was necessary for A to claim against the sub-contractor rather than B. See further Section 10.3.

Questions

1 Explain why the Sale of Goods Act and the Supply of Goods and Services Act were passed.
2 Which of the following contracts would be subject to the Sale of Goods Act and which to the Supply of Goods and Services Act?
  (a) A contract for a hundred tons of coal to be delivered in six weeks at a price of £85 a ton.
  (b) A contract to install air-conditioning in a theatre.
  (c) A contract for the hire of an industrial crane for nine months.
  (d) A contract for the produce from ten fields of barley with a price to be fixed in relation to the market prices at the time of harvest and paid for by cheque.

(e) A contract to part-exchange a fleet of six old company cars for six new ones.

Why is it important to know which Act the contracts are subject to?

3 Explain in your own words what is meant by 'merchantable quality'. Can you think of a better definition to describe the quality that could reasonably be expected when goods are supplied in a contract?

4 What are the four rules which determine when property is transferred in specific goods if this is not made clear in the contract?

5 When does the risk of loss shift from seller to buyer? What implications does this rule have for a business's insurance cover?

6 What is the *nemo dat* rule, and what are the main exceptions to it?

7 X Company order 1000 sheets of 2440mm × 1200mm × 12mm plywood from Y Company. When it arrives it is found to vary from 11mm to 13mm and the quality is not what was expected.
What are the rights of X Company in this situation? How could Y Company protect themselves?
Would your answer differ if the discrepancies were only noticed when the wood had been machined?

8 The buyer for Browns plc visits a trade fair and sees a model of a new piece of machinery manufactured by Greens Ltd. She is very impressed and orders four machines. The first piece of machinery is delivered and is satisfactory. However, the second is two months later than the delivery date stated, and the third is destroyed in a freak flood while being transported to Browns' Bristol factory by an independent third-party carrier. Browns now want to cancel the order for the fourth piece of machinery and are refusing to pay for the third which they claim was not their responsibility.
Advise Browns and Greens.

9 Joe runs an antiques shop and while browsing through the local market he comes across a silver plate which he thinks could be polished up and sold at a substantial profit. He buys the plate, and after renovation displays it in his window. He is dismayed to receive a visit from the local police force who state that the plate was stolen and has been identified by the original owner. Explain Joe's legal position.

Chapter 6

Standard-Form Contracts

'Standard-Form Contracts' is the term used to denote pre-printed documents which contain a set of standard contractual terms and conditions. These terms govern most contracts entered into by commercial concerns as they will be printed on the back of purchase orders, confirmation notes and the like. For this reason they are often known as back-of-order conditions. This leaves only the particular details of each contract, such as price and delivery date, to be negotiated and included elsewhere in the documentation, perhaps on the front of the form. An example of such a standard-form contract is shown below but other examples are readily available. Of course, all the laws of contract stated in the previous two chapters apply to such contracts as these documents are purely an efficient means of producing contracts *en masse*.

This chapter will consider the growth in popularity of these documents, the interpretation of the terms which are frequently found included in them, and the occasional problem which is caused by their use in the so-called 'battle of the forms'.

6.1　Why Are Standard-Form Contracts used?

The growth of the popularity and frequent use of standard-form contracts follow in the wake of the industrial revolution. As mechanisation of industry led to mass production, so it became unnecessary and wasteful to negotiate each contract for the supply of these goods individually. Mass-produced contracts were appropriate for mass-produced goods, and of course this also worked out less expensive in terms of negotiating time and expertise. It also seemed to be worthwhile to make use of such contracts because it meant that all foreseeable contingencies could be catered for within the standard terms. The great advantage of this is in planning and costing an enterprise. Instead of waiting for

TERMS AND CONDITIONS OF SALE

1. Acceptance of Order and Expiry Date. Orders are accepted only upon and subject to the Seller's Conditions of Sales as printed herein. Unless expressly accepted in writing any qualification of these conditions by the Buyer in any written or printed document or otherwise shall be inapplicable. Unless previously withdrawn Seller's quotation expires twenty-one days after the date thereof. No binding contract shall be created by the acceptance on the part of the Buyer of a quotation or offer made by the Seller until notice of the accepting of the order in writing shall have been given by the Seller.

2. Delivery. Any date named by the Seller for despatch or delivery is given and intended as an estimate only and is not to be of the essence of the contract. The Buyer shall nevertheless be bound to accept the goods ordered when available. The Seller shall not be liable in any way in respect of late despatch or delivery however caused nor shall such failure to despatch be deemed to be a breach of the contract. Where drawings specifications instructions and materials are to be supplied the Buyer shall supply the same in reasonable time to enable the Seller to despatch within the period named. Unless otherwise stated goods shall be sent carriage paid by rail or road transport at goods rate.

3. Prices. Orders are accepted on condition that goods will be invoiced at the prices ruling at the date of despatch. The Seller reserves the right to alter prices without notice to cover variations in the cost of raw materials labour etc. or through the Buyer's change of design or for any other reason. If variation in price occurs during the currency of an order the price of the undespatched portion of the order outstanding at the date of such variation in price shall be adjustd accordingly.

4. Terms of Business. Unless otherwise stated prices quoted are nett and accounts are due for payment monthly; the Seller reserves the right to charge interest at Bank Rate plus 1% on all overdue accounts, and further reserves the right to charge in full for all packing cases or cartons if not returned within three calendar months from the date of invoice in servicable condition carriage paid to our Works. Non-returnable packing may be charged for.

5. Warranties. Whilst the Seller will endeavour to execute orders in accordance therewith all conditions guarantees or warranties including guarantees or warranties as to quality or description of the goods or their life or wear or their use under any conditions whether known or made known to the Seller or not and whether expressed or implied by statute or common law are hereby excluded. Whilst the utmost care is taken to ensure the accuracy of the information and data furnished to customers the sale of goods produced by the Seller is subject to the condition that the Seller will not in any circumstances be liable for injuries losses expenses or damage direct indirect or consequential sustained by the Buyer which may in any degree be attributable to the adoption either by the Buyer or by any third party of technical information data or advice given by or on behalf of the Seller in relation to the use of its goods.

6. Force Majeure. Should delivery of any of the goods sold be prevented or delayed by happenings or occurrences due to 'force majeure' or by reason of mobilisation hostilities acts of Queen's enemies or war (whether declared or not) Government action department instructions or act of God riots combination of workmen lockouts strikes or disturbances wherever taking place want of raw materials or fuel in consequence of non-delivery or any other causes want or railway trucks accidents fire flood blocking of or accidents to shipping or railway lines failure of steamers to sail at advertised time reduction or stoppage of output at the Works where the goods are being manufactured through flood fire heat frost holidays breakdowns of or accidents to machinery or any other causes or any circumstances whatever beyond the Seller's control the Seller reserves the right to cancel or suspend deliveries. In any event the Seller shall not be liable in any way for loss or damage arising directly or indirectly through or in consequence of such events or happenings.

7. Shortages Damage and/or Loss in Transit. No claim for non-delivery of part of a consignment or for damage in transit corrosion shortage of delivery deviation delay or detention will be entertained unless a separate notice in writing is given to the carrier concerned and to the Seller within three days and a complete claim in writing is made to the Seller within five days of receipt of the goods. In the case of non-delivery of a whole consignment notice in writing must be given to the carrier concerned and to the Seller within ten days and a complete claim in writing made within a further ten days of the date of despatch. Where goods are accepted without being checked the delivery book of the carrier concerned must be signed 'not examined'. The goods in respect of which any such claim is made shall be preserved intact as delivered for a period of fourteen days from notification of the claim within which time the Seller and the carrier shall have the right to attend at the Buyer's works to investigate the complaint. Any breach of this condition shall disentitle the Buyer to any allowance in respect of the claim.

8. Tests and Inspection. Unless otherwise agreed all testing and inspection specified by the Buyer or implied by the order or customary to the Seller's practice shall be at the Seller's works and shall be final.

9. Defective Goods. Goods represented by the Buyer to be defective or not to conform to contract and returned to and accepted by the Seller as such will be replaced as originally ordered if required and practicable or will be credited but shall not form the subject of any claim for work done by the Buyer transport costs consequential damages or expenses loss of profit on or any claim arising through re-sale or any other loss damage or expense whatsoever or howsoever incurred. No claim in respect of defective goods will be valid unless made and alleged defective goods returned within ninety days of the date of despatch of the goods nor will such claim be accepted as a reason for cancellation of the remainder of the order.

10. Infringement of Patents Registered Designs or Copyright. The buyer shall indemnify the Seller against all damages penalties costs and expenses to which the Seller may become liable as a result of work done in accordnace with the Buyer's specification which involves infringement or alleged infringement of a patent registered design or copyright.

11. Buyer's Bankruptcy. If the Buyer shall make default in or commit any breach of any of his obligations to the Seller or if any distress or execution shall be levied upon the Buyer or if the Buyer shall offer to make any arrangement with creditors or commit any act of bankruptcy or if any petition in Bankruptcy shall be presented against him or if the Buyer is a limited company any resolution or petition to wind up such company's business (other than for the purposes of any amalgamation or reconstruction which becomes effective) shall be passed or presented the Seller shall have the right forthwith to determine by written notice posted to the Buyer any contract then subsisting without prejudice to any claim or right the Seller might otherwise make or exercise.

12. Default in Payment., Should default be made by the Buyer in paying any sum due under any contract as and when it becomes due or should the Buyer be in breach in any respect of the contract entered into the Seller shall have the right with or without notice in the discretion of the Seller either to suspend all further deliveries until the default be made good or to determine any contract then subsisting so far as any further goods remain to be delivered without prejudice to any claim or right the Seller might otherwise make or exercise.

13. Arbitration and Lex Loci. The construction validity and performance of this contract shall be governed by the law of England and any question dispute or difference which may arise under out of or in connection with or in relation to this order or contract or touching the meaning and construction of the same shall be referred to the arbitration of a person to be appointed failing agreement of the parties by the President for the time being of the Law Society of England and the decision of such arbitrator shall be binding on both parties and shall be a submission to arbitration within the meaning of the Arbitration Act 1950 or any re-enactment or statutory modification thereof for the time being in force.

14. Reservation of Title
    (a) The risk in the goods shall pass to the Buyer upon delivery, but ownership thereof shall remain in the Seller until payment in full has been made (each order being considered as a whole) or the Buyer resells the goods as provided herein.
    (b) Before payment in full is made, the Buyer shall have power to resell the goods (as principal towards sub-purchaser but as agent between Buyer and Seller) and the Seller shall be beneficially entitled to and the Buyer shall be under fiduciary duty to account to the Seller for the proceeds of resale and any claim thereto.
    (c) If the Buyer, not having made payment in full for the goods, mixes them with other goods or uses them in the manufacture of other products, the ownership of the other goods or products shall thereupon vest in the Seller as security for such payment, and accordingly sub-clause (b) shall as far as appropriate apply to such other goods or products.
    (d) Until such payment in full the Buyer shall clearly identify the goods or the said other goods or products as being the property of the Seller.
    (e) The Seller shall be entitled forthwith to recover and resell any or all of such goods or products to which the Seller has title hereunder and to enter upon the premises of the Buyer with such transport as may be necessary for that purpose, if the Buyer commits any default hereunder with expression shall without prejudice to the generality thereof include failure to pay the Seller on the due date, the appointment of a receiver of the Buyer's business or the presentation of a petition to wind up the Buyer. Nothing herein shall entitle the Buyer to return the goods or to refuse or delay payment for them.

Reproduced with permission

problems to arise and then having to solve them later, perhaps even having to resort to the courts for a settlement, as much as possible can be dealt with in advance in the contract itself. Then if a problem arises, the solution is to be found by referring to the contract. All likely costs can therefore be calculated in the planning stage. Two types of clause which are particularly useful for this are *force majeure* and liquidated damages clauses (see below).

However, in order to take full advantage of these benefits, it is necessary for businesses to ensure that their own terms and conditions are carefully drafted to apply in exactly the way intended. Even more importantly, once this is accomplished, it must be ensured that these terms are presented in such a way that they will form the basis of the contracts that are entered into. This is not always possible, but an understanding of the legal principles governing the situation will help in ensuring that these terms apply in the majority of cases.

An alternative to having one contract that is used in all circumstances is to negotiate separate standard forms with each of the most important suppliers or customers of a particular business on an individual basis, to avoid the problems involved and to ensure the relationship is built on a solid foundation.

6.2   Does the Set of Standard Terms Form Part of the Contract?

In a case involving a set of printed terms which were included on a 'sold note' and left for the business buyers but never read by them, the court decided that if the terms were presented in such a way that a normal prudent business person would assume that they included terms of the contract, then such terms would form part of that contract. (*Roe v R.A. Naylor Ltd.* [1918] 87 L.J.K.B. 958.) Factors which would be relevant here include the style of printing and position of the terms. Most business people are familiar with the small feint print on the back of invoices, etc. and would expect the terms to be included there. However, judges recently have begun to question the use of very small illegible print and the use of complex, legalistic language, and it may be that a decision could disallow a set of terms for this reason. But this is most likely only to apply to exclusion clauses where the legislation obliges the judges to test the 'reasonableness' of such terms (see Section 6.4 below).

It has long been established that if a written contract is signed, the contents will be binding on the signing party regardless of whether it has been read or the contents understood, unless they have been misrepresented. On the other hand a court has held that a binding oral promise can override the printed terms if there is sufficient evidence of such a promise.

It may even be the case that a document which arrives after the contract has been completed may be incorporated in the contract if such terms had always been used in the previous course of dealings. It will then be held that it was implied that such terms would form a part of the present contract; the fact that the confirmation note or invoice, etc. including these terms did not arrive until negotiations were complete did not prevent that contract including those terms. This situation must be distinguished from 'past consideration' (see Section 4.7(*b*)), where completely new terms are introduced after agreement has been reached.

The necessity to be aware of the contents of such sets of terms cannot therefore be stressed too strongly, and if they appear unacceptable an attempt should be made to negotiate them out of that particular deal. Should it be decided that this is commercially unacceptable, then the consequences of accepting these terms should be realised and allowed for, perhaps by arranging insurance to cover the potential loss. The implications of these clauses are dealt with below.

6.3 Whose Standard-Form Governs the Contract – 'The Battle of the Forms'.

In circumstances where only one party to the transaction is using a standard-form contract, it will be fairly clear that those are the terms which go to make up the contract, provided the requirements of Section 6.2 above are met. However, as has been said, most large companies will make use of standard-forms and this leads to the situation where both sides despatch forms purporting to be the terms and conditions of the contract. It is highly unlikely that the two sets will be identical or even similar, as the purchaser's form may provide that the price is fixed, while the seller's form allows for a price variation, for example. So which form prevails? The answer to the question will normally be found by applying the rules of offer, counter offer and acceptance to the various documents. (See Section 4.5(*a*) above.) This may mean that the party who sent the last document will win the battle, applying the 'last-shot' doctrine. But this relies on the other party performing the contract, which is taken as an implied acceptance of the last set of terms. Before this is done therefore, no contract will have been made and so either side can withdraw and incurs no penalties.

Most organisations take the precaution of including a term such as:

'All orders are accepted only upon and subject to the seller's conditions of sale as printed herein. Any qualification or variation of these conditions by the buyer in any written or printed document or otherwise shall be inapplicable.'

If both parties include such a term, this may lead the courts to conclude that no contract had ever been made as no agreement had been reached, and therefore only a reasonable sum could be recoverable for work done. However, the courts will be very reluctant to reach this conclusion as this is clearly not the intention of the parties. It should be noted that this did not help the sellers in the *Ex-cello* case as they had included such a term in their conditions, but were still bound by the buyers' terms because they had returned an acknowledgement slip (see Section 4.5).

Obviously it is essential that such a step is avoided, and as a precautionary measure each piece of paper despatched by businesses should reiterate that the contract is made subject to their own terms and conditions. To be absolutely safe it may be necessary to print these in full wherever practicable. It has even been suggested that expeditors in the buying department should be instructed not to 'chase' orders which have not materialised over the telephone, because by doing so they may be accepting the last set of terms if the supplier had got in the 'last shot'. However, it is accepted that this may not be commercially viable.

It is, of course, as always, open to the parties to ignore the strict legal position and negotiate a settlement should a problem arise. However, to do this would be to have wasted the time spent in carefully drafting the standard set of terms in the first place. On the other hand, a party without a standard-form which he can at least argue forms the basis of the contract would be in a very much weaker bargaining position than the other. It is for this reason that it is often concluded that though there is no guaranteed way of winning the battle of the forms, care can at least be taken so as not to lose it!

The content of the set of standard terms is obviously also important. Not all the clauses to be examined in the following

Sections will be found in every standard-form contract. However, they appear very frequently, and it is important that their meaning and implications are understood.

6.4 Exclusion/Exemption/Limitation Clauses

These clauses are probably the most common of all to be found in a contract, particularly that emanating from a seller or supplier. Such a clause will attempt to completely exclude or at least limit the liability of the supplier of goods or services for any breach or variation of the contract. It is very common for sellers to limit their liability for providing faulty or defective products to the cost of the goods only, so that any resulting damage cannot be compensated for. They will almost always completely exclude the implied terms in the Sale of Goods Act or other appropriate legislation (see Section 5.3 above). An example of an exclusion clause is as follows:

> The Company's liability under any order is limited to replacement or remedial work under these conditions of sale, to the entire exclusion of any other remedy which, but for this condition, the buyer might have. Any representation, condition, warranty or other undertaking in relation to the contract whether express or implied by statute, common law, custom or otherwise and whether made or given before or after the date of the order or acceptance thereof, is hereby excluded for all purposes. Save as provided in these conditions, the Company shall be under no liability of any sort (however arising) and shall not in any circumstances be liable for any damage, injury, direct or consequential or other loss or loss of profits or costs, charges and expenses, howsoever arising.

How effective are such clauses? Until 1977 the courts had very little option but to enforce them, provided that they were clearly part of the contract, although they always interpreted them very strictly against the party seeking to rely on them. In 1977 with the introduction of the Unfair Contract Terms Act they were given legislative power to challenge such clauses.

The Act applies to the exclusion of business liability and it has three main provisions.

(a) Section 2 prohibits the exclusion in any circumstances of liability for causing death or personal injury to others through negligence. Any attempt to do so by means of a contract term or use of a notice has no effect. This does not mean that the other party will necessarily be liable for there will still be the requirement

to prove negligence (for what this entails see further Section 10.3): it only means that a business cannot excuse itself from liability. There is, however, no penalty attached to the continued use of such clauses, and though totally invalid they can still sometimes be seen and may be sufficient to deter an uninformed injured party.

Section 2 goes on to state that the exclusion of other liability caused by negligence, for example damage to property, is subject to the reasonableness test (see below).

(b) *Section 3* only applies when a business is dealing with another business on a standard-form contract or with a consumer (for how this is defined for the purposes of this Act, see Section 5.4 above). This states that any attempt to limit liability for breach of a contract or to exclude liability for performing something different from or not performing what was promised in the contract is also subject to the reasonableness test.

An interesting point to raise here is whether a business which has negotiated out one or two clauses from the set of standard terms could then claim that the contract was still a standard-form contract and therefore challenge a remaining exclusion or limitation clause on that basis. Where the contract has been individually negotiated, it is clear that no objection can be made to an exclusion or limitation clause, unless the contract is with a consumer.

(c) *Section 6* of the Act deals with the implied terms and has been discussed in Section 5.4 above.

(d) *Section 11* contains the reasonableness test. In the case of terms in a contract which are subject to the reasonableness test, the standard they are judged by is whether they were reasonable clauses to have included in the contract at the time the contract was made, bearing in mind the knowledge of the parties at the time.

Judged by this, if the clause was held to be reasonable then it will be valid and therefore it would absolve the party relying on it from liability to the extent that this is covered by the term. If the clause is declared to be unreasonable it will have no effect at all and the question of liability will be determined on the normal principles of contract law.

There are further guidelines to help the courts decide when a clause is reasonable, but these are said to apply only in relation to exclusion of the implied terms. However, it would seem that the courts will bear them in mind whenever they have to determine reasonableness. The first and probably the most important of the guidelines, refers to the relative bargaining position of the parties. Obviously a large multi-national company which negotiates with a sole trader is in a far more powerful position and may have been able to impose its terms on the other, in which case the court may well decide that the clause was unreasonable in the circumstances. Between two multi-nationals, or two sole traders, the decision may well be reversed. Other guidelines include the possibility of the other party going elsewhere and getting better terms, and whether they should have been aware of the existence and implications of the term. It is the party who seeks to rely on the clause who must prove that it is reasonable.

One of the few decided cases on this point will help to illustrate this rule. In *George Mitchell* v *Finney Lock Seeds* [1983] 2 A.C. 803, the House of Lords considered several factors to be relevant when deciding whether a clause in a seed supplier's contract which restricted liability for delivering faulty or, as in this case, the wrong seeds to the cost of replacing the seeds was reasonable or not. These included the fact that neither the National Farmers' Union nor any buyers had ever objected to the term, although they were familiar with it as it was widely used, and the potential loss was extremely high – in the present case the cost of the seeds was about £200 while the damages sought were over £60 000 – and it might therefore have appeared reasonable to take steps to restrict liability. On the other hand, the wrong seeds could not have been delivered without negligence on the supplier's part, and they could have insured against that quite easily. In particular it was felt important that in the past the sellers had paid compensation over and above their contractual terms in circumstances where they thought it was a justified claim. This seemed to be the decisive factor in convincing the court that on balancing all these points the clause was on the whole unreasonable and therefore invalid. It was almost as though the sellers had proved that they themselves thought the clause unreasonable!

It is also worth noting that the practice of having onerous terms in the contract but not enforcing them backfired on the company in this case and suggests that it is advisable to draw up standard terms which can be relied on in practice. Another point to take from this and the other few cases that have reached the superior courts on reasonableness and exclusion clauses is that each clause will be looked at in the light of the individual contract and thus no hard-and-fast rules can be gleaned on how to draft an acceptable clause. Even Finney Lock's clause may be considered reasonable and therefore effective in different circumstances.

It should be noted that this decision was made on the basis of a differently worded definition of 'reasonableness', but it is unlikely that the court would have decided differently on the current wording. Unfortunately, so few cases have reached the courts on these provisions that the position is far from clear. As noted previously, however, this very uncertainty allows businesses to continue to use exemption clauses without any clear idea as to whether they are effective or not, but they can be relied on when negotiating a settlement with the other parties for the reason that neither will relish the idea of testing the clause in court.

The Unfair Contract Terms Act is misleadingly named as it does not only apply to contract terms and it also does not deal with all unfair clauses in contracts. It must be stressed that only clauses covered by the 1977 Act, i.e. exclusion or limitation clauses, can be put to the reasonableness test by the court. All other clauses (with one or two very rare exceptions involving unfair influence) can be as unfair and unreasonable as the parties choose – in the interests of freedom of contract the courts will enforce the clause if they feel that it was validly included in the contract, does not contravene the law and has been 'accepted' by the other party.

6.5   *Force Majeure* Clauses

Force majeure clauses are used for practical reasons as a way of planning for contingencies, and for legal reasons to avoid the restrictive view that the courts take of the doctrine of frustration (see Section 4.10). Traditionally, the courts are only prepared to say that a contract is frustrated, thus releasing both parties from further obligations under it, if it is now impossible to perform and not merely commercially more difficult.

To avoid being taken to court for breach of contract and not establishing the defence of frustration, companies often write into their contract circumstances which they consider will be sufficient to bring the contract to an end. In such an eventuality, the contract will be ended by agreement, rather than frustration.

An example of a *force majeure* clause is as follows:

Strikes, lockouts, labour disturbances, policies or restrictions of governments, or any other contingency whatsoever beyond sellers control, including war, to be sufficient excuse for any delay or non-fulfilment traceable to any of these causes.

As shown, it usually contains a list of circumstances such as war, epidemics and strikes which are beyond the parties' control and are considered sufficient to end or suspend the contract. Most prudent companies will also go on to cover the financial consequences of such an ending of the contract. The exact circumstances of when such a clause would come into play may need to be settled by arbitration.

6.6   Liquidated Damages Clauses

Liquidated damages clauses prevent the necessity of going to court to determine the measure of damages which are payable when a breach of contract occurs. They set out in advance the amount to be paid if a particular eventuality occurs, and are used particularly to penalise late performance of a contract where a certain sum can become payable for each week, month, etc. that performance is delayed. An example of such a clause is as follows:

> The contractor shall pay the building owner £150 per week or part thereof for delay in completion of the works.

Liquidated damages clauses are often referred to in a contract as penalties, or penalty clauses. However, this is a misnomer because liquidated damages clauses are only enforceable if they are *not* penalties. They can be challenged if the party who has to pay the money claims the amount was not a 'genuine pre-estimate of loss' but was put in as a penalty to force him into performing the contract correctly. If this is accepted by the court, then the clause is disregarded and damages assessed as usual. See Section 4.11(*a*).

On the other hand, if the clause is not a penalty, then only the amounts stated in the clause can be recovered. So if it is estimated that the loss occasioned by each week's delay in say, completion of building work, would be £100 per week and this is included in the contract which is subsequently six weeks behind schedule, the loss recoverable will be £600 regardless of whether the actual loss was £60 or £6000. (In the former case of course, the clause may well be challenged as a penalty, but it is most unlikely to be so in the latter case!) Thus any drafter of such clauses must be careful to estimate as accurately as possible what loss such breaches would occasion. If there is an over-estimate the clauses may be challenged which nullifies the point of using them in the first place, but if there is an under-estimation the company will lose out. But at least the time and expense of going to court will have been avoided and such clauses can be very useful in concentrating the supplier's mind on performing the contract on time.

6.7   Romalpa or Retention of Title Clauses

These clauses are named after the case in which such a clause was first successfully used, *Aluminium Industrie Vaassen B.V.* v *Romalpa Aluminium Ltd.* [1976] 2 All E.R. 552. An example of the type of clause involved is as follows:

> The property in the goods shall not pass to the Buyer until the Buyer has paid to the Seller the whole price thereof. If, notwithstanding that the property in the goods has not passed to the Buyer, the Buyer shall sell the goods in such a manner as to pass to a third party a valid title to the goods, the Buyer shall hold the proceeds of such sale on trust for the Seller. The Buyer agrees that prior to the payment of the whole price of the goods the Seller may at any time enter the Buyer's premises and remove the goods therefrom and that prior to such payment the Buyer shall keep the goods separate and identifiable for this purpose. Notwithstanding that property in the goods shall not pass to the Buyer save as above, the goods shall be at the risk of the Buyer from the time of collection by or delivery to him of the goods.

Many companies include a clause in similar terms in the hope that in the eventuality of the buyer going into liquidation before having paid for the goods, some at least of the loss can be recovered without having to wait for the liquidator to share the assets, if any (see Section 3.5). Depending on the way in which the clause is phrased, it will probably be possible to recover any unused goods which remain on the buyer's premises and can be identified as the seller's. However, difficulties arise if the goods have been incorporated into other goods, even if they can still be identified, for example brakes in a new car. The courts have to decide whether the Romalpa clause gives the seller any right over the final end-product, in the example above the car, and even over the proceeds of goods if they had already been sold to a sub-buyer.

In circumstances where the goods are sold to a sub-buyer in their original state and the contract has made it clear that the proceeds of such sale must be held on the original seller's behalf in a separate account and this has been complied with, it may be possible to recover such money before it is submerged in the total assets of the liquidated company. However, if the goods have been incorporated into others, it has been decided that the original sellers lose any rights of ownership over their property, but the clause may create what is known as a 'charge' over the goods in their new form. But in order to enforce this charge it needs to be registered under the Companies Act 1985 section 395 and it is highly unlikely that companies would do this in the case of all their contracts including such a clause. It would then appear that any rights over the goods or the proceeds of their sale are lost and the original seller is simply in the same position as any other unsecured creditor.

This would appear to be the situation as the result of several decisions following after the *Romalpa* case. It must be stressed that the exact position will depend on the wording of the clause and the circumstances of the sale of the goods. It has been suggested that very often in a liquidation, the liquidator will get together all the unpaid suppliers who have Romalpa clauses in their contracts and suggest that if it is necessary to argue about who owns what the situation will never be resolved, and perhaps they would all like to drop their claims. However, major creditors may feel that their losses will be such that it is worth pursuing the matter through the courts. For the position where no retention of title clause is used, see Section 5.5.

6.8 Arbitration Clauses

Businesses may prefer disputes to be dealt with by arbitration for many reasons, as set out in Section 2.5, and it is common practice to include a clause to this effect in their contract. Thus, if despite all the careful planning in the rest of the contract an irresolvable dispute arises between the parties, the matter can be disposed of with hopefully less bother than going to court. An example of an arbitration clause is as follows:

> If any dispute, difference or question shall at any time hereafter arise between the parties in respect of or in connection with the present contract, the same shall be referred to the arbitration of a person to be agreed upon by the parties, or failing agreement, to be nominated by . . . in accordance with the Arbitration Acts 1950 and 1979.

The arbitration clause will normally state who the arbitrator will be or the method by which he or she will be appointed. Such a clause may be referred to as a *Scott* v *Avery* clause as this case decided that a dispute over a contract that included an arbitration clause had to go to arbitration first, and there could not be a direct appeal to the courts. The 1979 Arbitration Act allows only two grounds for appeal to court for a form of judicial review after the case has been heard. These are if both parties desire it or if one party plus the High Court certify that there is a point of law involved which will substantially affect the rights of the parties. Otherwise the 'award' made by the arbitrator is final and can be enforced in the same way as a court's judgement. It is also possible to contract out of the right to go to court at all in the case of a non-domestic dispute, i.e. one involving companies not based in this country, but where the parties are domestic it is only possible to agree not to appeal when a dispute has begun.

Questions

1 What do you understand by the term 'standard-form contract'?
2 Account for the increased use of standard-form contracts.
3 What are the advantages and disadvantages of standard-form contracts for
   (a) large businesses?
   (b) small businesses?
   (c) consumers?
4 What do you understand by the term 'Battle of the Forms'? Why might it be important to win such a battle, and can this be guaranteed?
5 Why was the Unfair Contract Terms Act passed? Briefly outline its main provisions.
6 Why is it necessary to take care when drafting a liquidated damages clause?
7 What is a Romalpa Clause and why are such clauses so common in standard-form contracts?
8 Collect as many examples as you can of standard-form contracts and try to identify the types of clauses mentioned in the previous chapter.

Chapter 7

Agency

Businesses use agents in various forms throughout their business activities, particularly if they are companies as all companies must have human agents to act on their behalf. Agents may be employees of the company, such as managing directors or sales managers, or they may be independent outsiders hired for a specific purpose because they possess a particular expertise, such as solicitors, employment agencies, or shipping agents. What they have in common is the power to alter the position of the party they are acting for, known as the principal, and bring them into contractual arrangements with a third party. This chapter will examine how agents obtain their authority to act, the exact nature of the relationship between the three parties involved–the principal, agent and third party–and in what circumstances the company is bound by actions of those acting on its behalf. Most of the law in this area is based on well established precedents set in the nineteenth century and the principles still apply in modern commercial situations.

It is perhaps worth mentioning that, confusingly, some use of the term agents in commercial situations does not denote that an agency relationship in law exists. For example motor agents are usually independent of the manufacturer and are therefore not acting as their agents.

7.1   The Agent's Role

The essence of the agency arrangement is that the agent acts as a go-between to bring the principal and the third party together as contracting parties. The normal rule in contract, known as the privity rule, see Section 4.7(d), is that only the party to enter into the contract will be bound by it. Agency is an exception because the principal in effect 'steps into the shoes' of the agent once the deal has been negotiated and takes over all the rights and obligations under the contract, leaving the agent with none. Normally, there will be another pre-existing contract between the principal and agent which authorises the agent to enter into negotiations, although this is not always the case, see Section 7.2 below. Again, occasionally, the agent incurs personal liability on the contract and is therefore contractually bound to the third party (see Section 7.5), but this is unusual.

7.2   The Agent's Authority

The agent achieves the power to alter the position of the principal in one of four ways outlined below:

(a) *Express authority*

This is achieved by appointment, which may be made in writing or orally. Along with the expressly stated powers that the agent acquires go a series of 'implied' powers without which it would be impossible for commercial life to continue. Thus an agent appointed for a particular purpose will not be expressly told everything that she or he can do, for it will be assumed that certain authority which always applies to such agents has been granted. Should the principal wish to restrict this implied or usual authority of the agent, it must be made clear to all third parties whom the agent may contact, otherwise the principal will still be bound by the contract made. For example, if the manager of a public house is expressly forbidden to buy spirits from anyone other than specified suppliers, but does so, the question of whether the principal will be bound by that contract will be answered by looking at what is normal in the trade. Were normal practice to be for managers to have unrestricted rights to order spirits, the principal would be bound unless the third party has been informed of the restriction. On the other hand, if normal practice is for selected suppliers to be used only, and the third party knew he was not one of these, then the principal would not be bound by the contract.

This may appear at first sight to be unfair and almost unworkable if a principal does wish to restrict the authority of the agent and has to inform every potential third party of this fact. However, if the rule were the other way then commerce would collapse, because no third party would be willing to deal with an agent, fearing that he or she did not have full authority. The principal is in the best position to control the situation by only employing trustworthy agents, who will not disobey instructions. If need be, the principal can also take action against his own agent for breach of the contract between them.

(b) *Ostensible or Apparent Authority*

In circumstances where a principal makes it appear as though someone has authority to act as an agent and a third party relies on this, then the principal will be bound by any contract made between the supposed agent and third party, even though in fact the agent has no such authority at all. So in a case involving a company secretary who hired cars in the name of the company, but which were in fact for his own use, the company was bound by the contract to the third party. Simply by appointing a company secretary it was making it appear to outsiders that certain authority would have been given to the man: *Panorama Developments Ltd.* v *Fidelis Furnishing Fabrics Ltd.* [1971] 2 Q.B. 711.

The difference between this and the implied or usual authority of an agent is that the latter is an extension of actual authority that has been granted. The former arises when no authority has been given at all, but it appears that it has. Again, the way for principals to guard against being caught by this rule is to ensure that all those who appear to have authority are responsible people and will not abuse their position. One practical suggestion is to keep control over those who can write letters on official headed stationery.

(c) *Ratification*

Authority is granted in this situation where at the time the contract in question was entered into, no such power existed. In other words, this is giving retrospective authority to an agent to act on behalf of a principal and might arise either where the supposed agent had no authority to act at the time or was exceeding the authority that had been granted. In order that this cannot work unfairly against the interests of third parties, stringent conditions have to be met before a principal can ratify the act of an agent.

Firstly, the principal must be in existence at the time the contract was entered into, for example it must not be a company that has not yet been formed, as in the case of *Kelner* v *Baxter* [1866] L.R. 2 C.P. 174. Also the principal must have had the capacity to make such a contract, i.e. was not a minor, or insane, or an enemy alien. It must be disclosed that the supposed agent is acting on someone else's behalf – another party cannot step into the contract at some later date unexpectedly – and the principal must know of all the relevant circumstances at the time of ratification. Provided these conditions are met, the contract will become binding on third party and principal from the time that it was originally made. This means in effect that only the proposed principal has the chance to refuse to be bound by the contract if he or she does not wish to ratify it.

(d) Emergency

Occasionally, but not very frequently nowadays owing to increasingly sophisticated methods of communication, someone may take action in an emergency situation on behalf of another party without having existing authority. She or he may then claim to have been acting as an agent and therefore not be personally bound by any contract entered into for the benefit of the 'principal'. This will only be the case, however, in a genuine emergency, when it is impossible to contact the principal for instructions and the action is taken in the best interests of the principal and not just for the convenience of the agent. For instance, where a station master sold off a consignment of tomatoes during a rail strike he was held liable for the loss suffered as a result. The owners showed that they could have arranged for the fruit to travel by road to London where because of the strike they could have got a far higher price.

7.3   Relationship between Agent and Principal

There are certain terms implied in the contractual agreement between the principal and agent because of the special nature of the relationship. This is described as being of 'the utmost good faith'. Thus, fairly obviously, the agent must not accept bribes from third parties but if she or he does, this must be accounted for to the principal in addition to any loss suffered as a result. Alternatively, the principal would be able to recover this from the third party and avoid the contract which had been made between them. Although this may seem no more than would be expected, those who receive a little 'gift' at Christmas from suppliers and others might be interested to know that the principal does not have to show that there was a corrupt motive involved, nor that the 'bribe' had influenced the agent's actions. It is also worth pointing out that such behaviour would probably justify instant dismissal (see further Section 14.2) and potential criminal prosecution.

At a less culpable level, the agent is obliged to account to the principal for any secret profit gained as a result of being the principal's agent. This may not necessarily be because the principal has suffered a loss, but any property or information gleaned as a result of acting on behalf of the principal is in theory the principal's property.

The agent is also obliged not to allow a conflict of interest to arise, for example, by acting for both third party and principal without disclosure, or by selling his or her own property to the principal without disclosure; and confidential information must not be passed on. The agent must also not delegate the authority which has already been delegated by the principal to someone else, unless this has been expressly agreed or is for purely administrative acts or is common practice in that area. Even so the agent would be liable to the principal for the activities of such sub-agents.

The agent is also under the normal obligation found in contracts of service (and now codified in the Supply of Goods and Services Act, see Section 5.11) to act with reasonable care and skill. This would include following the principal's instructions exactly, even if this would work to the principal's disadvantage. If these instructions are unclear, the agent would be obliged to act in the best possible interests of the principal.

The principal is under a duty to pay the agent a reasonable sum for his or her services if none has been agreed and to indemnify the agent for any legitimate costs occasioned on behalf of the principal.

7.4   Relationship between Principal and Third Party

This is the crux of the arrangement brought about as a result of the agency agreement. Normally, if all goes as intended, the principal and third party will be contractually bound to one another. Provided the agent has completely fulfilled all the principal's instructions and has fully disclosed the existence of the principal on whose behalf he or she is acting, and has acted within his or her authority, the agent is no longer involved.

Occasionally, however, the principal and third party will not be fully bound and there is a question as to who can sue and be sued. This may arise for instance if the agent has now disclosed that he or she is acting on someone else's behalf, or has not made it clear who the principal is. In these situations it is necessary to consider all the circumstances to determine if the agent or the principal or both may be liable to the third party, and whether conversely the principal could claim against the third party.

Where the principal is undisclosed, i.e. the agent has not made it clear that someone else is involved, the third party has the option whether to claim against the agent or the principal, if neither is prepared to fulfill the contract, but must choose which to take action against and cannot claim against both. On the other hand, the undisclosed principal can step in and claim against the unsuspecting third party if the third party breaks the contract, but only in circumstances where the third party would not be unduly disadvantaged. (Note that this would not be possible if the principal was trying to ratify the agreement.) When the agent has pretended that he or she is the one and only principal, particularly if this is confirmed in writing, the principal may not be able to step in, and would have to be content with proceeding against the agent. Similarly, if the contract which has been made relies heavily on the identity of the parties involved, such as an employment contract, an unidentified principal could not take action against the third party. In *Said* v *Butt* [1920] 3 K.B. 497, a theatre critic who had been refused admittance to a theatre asked a friend as his agent to buy a ticket for the first night on his behalf, but was again legitimately refused admittance as the identity of the principal was material to this contract.

7.5   Relationship between Agent and Third Party

The best protection for an agent to avoid being made personally liable under a contract in circumstances outlined above, is to ensure that any document signed in his or her name is followed by the words 'as agent', 'as director', 'on behalf of' or whatever. But occasionally the agent may still be liable to the third party in circumstances where he or she has exceeded his or her authority, without the knowledge of the third party. This is so even if it is done under the mistaken belief that the principal will ratify the agreement later, or that such authority existed. The third party can then sue the agent for 'breach of warranty of authority', i.e. for falsely holding out that he or she had authority to make the contract in the first place. The third party is entitled to recover any actual loss as a result. Note that even where the agent had no authority, if the agreement is ratified by the principal, or the agent had apparent or usual authority, it is the principal and not the agent who is liable to the third party. See Section 7.2 above.

The agent may also be liable of course when the principal did not exist as in *Kelner* v *Baxter* – see Section 7.2 above, which rule is now confirmed in the Companies Act 1985, section 36 (4), or where the agent only pretended to act as an agent, and was in reality acting on his or her own behalf.

7.6   Ending Agency Agreements

The agency agreement ends in the same way as other contracts, i.e. when its terms have been fully carried out, or the contract is frustrated, or the principal withdraws authority. Authority cannot be withdrawn however where it is 'coupled with an interest'. This most often arises when the agent is granted the right to act as an agent in order to collect a debt owed by the principal to the agent. Here the agent has the right to have the agency arrangement continued until the debts are paid off. It can also end where either the principal or agent becomes insane, dies or becomes insolvent.

Questions

1 Why do businesses need to appoint agents? Give examples of various common types of agents.
2 How is an agency relationship created?
3 Explain to a newly appointed agent what his or her responsibilities to the principal are.
4 In what circumstances may an agent be liable to the third party?
5 What is meant by an undisclosed principal? Why do you think principals sometimes choose to remain undisclosed? What are the legal consequences of such secrecy?
6 A clerk in your company's warehouse, Joe, has always had the power to sign delivery notes when goods are delivered, but the procedure is changed and Joe is told that in future only the stores manager can do so. However, these instructions are ignored and further goods are accepted in this manner. Your company now wish to reject a consignment of faulty goods which have been accepted in this way. Advise them.
7 Paul asks Arlene to buy some fixtures and fittings at a price not exceeding £500 in total for a new shop which Paul is opening. Arlene phones only two companies and agrees to buy the items for £550 from the second company, Swizzles. Swizzles know Arlene acts as an agent in these matters, but does not bother to find out on this occasion who she is acting for. As the fixtures and fittings are difficult to obtain, Paul is prepared to accept

them at the higher price. However, he later finds that these are available from a well known supplier at £450 and refuses to accept the goods when Swizzles supplies them. Advise Paul, Arlene and Swizzles of their legal position.

Would your answer be different if it could be shown that Arlene had spent an all-expenses-paid holiday in the Caribbean with Swizzles' managing director two months ago?

PART III

LEGAL REGULATION OF THE MARKET PLACE

The preceding Part has shown how laws developed in the courts through the resolution of business disputes and were therefore closely based on existing commercial practices. Parliament on the whole did not attempt to interfere with this process, and simply helped to clarify matters now and again by putting together statutory codifications of the existing law, e.g. in the Sale of Goods Act. In a sense therefore business developed its own rules, based on the guiding principles of freedom of contract (see Section 4.1) and *caveat emptor* (let the buyer beware). However, in the 1950s the 'economic paternalism' movement began to emerge with the aim of achieving more equality between the stronger and weaker elements in the market place, both competitors and customers, in the interests of economic efficiency and society at large. This led to an unprecedented stream of legislation, much of it initiated by the consumer protection movement and yet more in the field of employment protection (see Part IV). These statutes now co-exist with the Common Law rules and form an important part of business law.

Chapter 8
Consumer Protection and Competition Policy

An important element in post-war attempts to regulate the market place identified in the introduction to this Part was the growth in the consumer protection movement on the one hand and the initiation of a policy to stimulate competition on the other. This chapter examines the results of these two policies and how they operate in the present day.

8.1 The Consumer Protection Movement

The consumer protection movement developed as a response to the changes which occurred in the industrialised nations after the Second World War. New products such as cars and plastics became widely available and people generally had more money or credit to spend on luxury items. At the same time businesses were growing larger too with the spread of supermarkets and the growth of multi-national companies, and more sophisticated marketing techniques were being used to sell their products. Individual consumers therefore began to feel vulnerable and unable to make the sort of informed decisions and choices that were necessary in a market dominated by the *caveat emptor* principle. They therefore banded together in various pressure groups. The best known British example is probably the Consumers' Association, publishers of the *Which?* magazines. Groups put pressure on the government to change unsatisfactory laws and give additional protection to small buyers of goods and services. This led to the setting up of the Molony Committee which reported in 1961 and recommended new legislation, including some on advertising (see the Trade Descriptions Act 1968, Section 9.2), hire-purchase (see Section 11.5), and safety (Section 10.7). These recommendations were very gradually introduced and will be dealt with where relevant later in this Part.

In 1973, which perhaps can be seen as the highpoint of the achievement of the consumer protection movement, several important reforms were made. There was the introduction of the small claims arbitration procedure in the county courts for claims, then of under £25, which helped individuals to enforce their new and existing civil law rights (see Section 2.4), and legislation which prohibited the exclusion of implied terms from consumer contracts (see Section 6.4). But perhaps the piece of legislation with most potential for improving trading standards generally was the somewhat grandiosely titled Fair Trading Act 1973.

8.2   The Director General of Fair Trading

The Fair Trading Act created a completely new post of Director General of Fair Trading (DGFT) and provided for a back-up staff which is known as the Office of Fair Trading (OFT). The person appointed was to have overall responsibility for promoting consumer protection and fair trading without being unduly biased towards the interests of consumers or of businesses. In the first annual report of the DGFT the then director said that the 'OFT should not be either a champion of consumers or a defender of trade and industry'. The post is filled on a five-year term and is non-political in that it does not change with each government. The current, and second, holder of the post is Sir Gordon Borrie.

The creation of the post was also important in that it brought together for the first time the control of competition policy and consumer protection under the same body. This recognised the fact that the two issues were complementary in that protection for the consumer also resulted from businesses being free of constraints created by monopoly power and restrictive practices (see Sections 8.6–8.8).

8.3   Fair Trading Act, Part II

Apart from the role of overall responsibility as a 'watchdog' for consumer protection, the DGFT was given specific powers. Under Part II of the Act, the DGFT has the responsibility of identifying unfair business practices which adversely affect the economic interests of consumers and referring such practices to another specially created body of between ten and fifteen members called the Consumer Protection Advisory Committee (CPAC) for full investigation. As a result of this enquiry the CPAC can recommend to the Secretary of State that a new criminal offence be created by way of the introduction of a statutory instrument. The idea was that this would be a quick method of banning harmful business practices which were relatively widespread without having to wait for the time necessary to introduce an entirely new statute. This procedure has not proved to be very successful, however, and only three new offences have been created in the thirteen years of the Act's life. These are:

(a) Using notices which purport to exclude the consumer's inalienable rights, i.e. notices such as *no refunds* which suggest that the buyer has no remedy even when the goods are unmerchantable or not as described, which is not the case (see Section 5.4).

(b) The placing of advertisements in small ads and elsewhere by traders suggesting that they are private sellers. All traders must now disclose that they are acting in the course of a business, either expressly or by implication through the use of the business name. Buyers should know therefore that they have the right to claim if the goods are unmerchantable (section 14 of the Sale of Goods Act only applies to goods sold in the course of a business) and perhaps will be more wary knowing the seller is a professional. In addition much of the criminal legislation, such as the Trade Descriptions Act, designed to control business standards, only applies to those acting in the course of a business and without this provision traders could escape detection by the enforcement body, the local Trading Standards department.

(c) Mail-order sellers may no longer hide behind anonymous box-office numbers, but must give their business name and address. This provision has never had to be implemented in court, and it was a much watered-down version of the protection that the DGFT had originally wanted to give to mail-order shoppers.

A last reference to the CPAC in 1978 on the practice of quoting VAT exclusive prices has never resulted in a regulation being passed. It is now generally considered that the whole Part II procedure has lapsed as it has proved to be too lengthy and difficult a process to implement, although it is still on the statute book and could be revived if circumstances demanded.

8.4   Fair Trading Act, Part III

The powers given to the DGFT in Part III of the Fair Trading Act have been more widely used. These allow the DGFT to identify individual traders who are persistently acting unfairly to their customers by breaking the criminal or civil law: e.g. through not fulfilling contracts in time or at all. There is no requirement for such breaches to have been the subject of court action. Such businesses can be asked to give written assurances that they will desist from such behaviour in future. If they refuse or persist in breach of the undertaking they can be ordered to comply by the county court, or in the case of a larger company, the Restrictive Practices Court.

Should this court order be broken, the trader is in contempt of court which is a serious criminal offence and would render the trader liable to a heavy fine or even a prison sentence, plus of course the bad publicity such a case would generate. This procedure has been used against over 400 mainly small traders by the end of 1986 and few court cases have been necessary. It is intended to act as an additional sanction against those who are prepared to ignore and risk the consequences of the existing law. Although it cannot deal with rogues who will go out of business before action can be taken against them, it can act as a general deterrent and an incentive to all in the business world to maintain higher standards.

8.5   Codes of Practice

The DGFT also has the responsibility under the Fair Trading Act to encourage trade associations to prepare codes of practice which their members should abide by. In recent years a great deal of emphasis has been placed on this form of self-regulation as the best method of maintaining high standards and protecting consumers. Although the DGFT has no statutory power to compel a trade association to prepare such a code, nor to authorise one that has been produced, any that acquire the backing of the OFT will appear to have more authority than those without. Over twenty such authorised codes now exist, many in the area of the provision of services which have caused problems in the past, such as motor dealing, dry cleaning, double glazing and funerals.

The codes are all drawn up to be tailor-made for the particular trade, which is one advantage they enjoy over legislation which must necessarily be very broad. Generally all lay down minimum standards that members of the association should reach in dealing with customers, particularly when dealing with complaints. Many include a private arbitration scheme that consumers can use if they have a complaint against a member, rather than having to go to court. It is argued that traders are more willing to abide by rules in codes as they were drawn up by their own representatives and not imposed on them by outsiders as are laws, and thus the spirit of the code is more likely to be honoured. There will also be a certain amount of peer-group pressure to ensure members comply with the code and thereby enhance the reputation of the industry as a whole.

However, the main disadvantage of these codes is that they only apply to trade association members, and there is no requirement for, say, all funeral directors to belong to the relevant association. In some industries, like travel, it is very difficult to survive if the trader does not belong to the trade association ABTA, but it is still not compulsory, and in other trades, e.g. footwear, membership is only about 60%. On the whole, those who do not belong to the associations tend to cause most problems anyway. Even when a trader is a member, the trade association has no real power to punish an offender. Although it could fine or expel a member as a last resort, this does not prevent the business from carrying on in exactly the same manner. Also, there is a natural disinclination for the association to appear too draconian against its own membership.

Thus, although consumers and participating traders have benefited through the promotion of codes of practice, it is now generally recognised that these should not be seen as a substitute for legislation when widespread control is necessary. For some time there has been discussion between the OFT and interested parties about the introduction of a legal duty to trade fairly, with what this constitutes being answered by reference to an appropriate code of practice. Such legislation may well be introduced in the near future. This would no doubt be welcomed by the consumer protection movement, which has not been very successful in recent years in promoting new legislation because of the prevailing idea that market forces are the best way of regulating the economy in the interests of both businesses and the consumer. This philosophy had led to increasing emphasis on the other aspect of the DGFT's rôle as overseer of competition policy.

8.6   Competition Policy

In conjunction with the Secretary of State for Trade and Industry the DGFT has overall responsibility for competition policy. Another consequence of the restructuring of post-war industry, the policy has never been as clear-cut or aggressive as that pursued in similar economies in Europe and the USA. It is generally concerned with ensuring that the market place is as free as possible from obstacles created by monopoly power, restrictive and anti-competitive practices. In addition to the OFT, this policy is put into effect by two further bodies, the Monopolies and Mergers Commission (MMC) and the Restrictive Practices Court.

8.7　The Monopolies and Mergers Commission

(a) Control of Monopolies. Although it has usually been the practice of UK governments to encourage companies to expand and grow in order to make them able to compete more effectively, especially with large foreign enterprises, it is recognised that if a company becomes too large it may cause problems for customers and competitors alike. For instance, it may neglect such matters as the quality and price of its goods and services if there is no alternative source available, and it may be able to quash any prospective new competitor by, for example, temporarily lowering its prices to an uneconomic level so that the newcomer has to withdraw. Therefore it is felt necessary to keep a watching brief on companies which could be in this position. To this end, the DGFT or the Secretary of State has the power to refer a company or group which control over 25% of any market (although not a monopoly in the true sense of the word) to an independent body of people, with experience of the commercial world, called the Monopolies and Mergers Commission for a full investigation of their activities. The purpose of the investigation is to discover if anything the company or companies do as a consequence of their powerful position can be said to 'operate against the public interest', for example by charging unjustifiably high prices or not distributing their goods or services fairly. There is no presumption that just because it is large it is necessarily harmful.

Due to the wide-ranging nature of the investigation, the MMC will take over two years to complete its enquiry, after which a report is submitted to the Secretary of State. This may result in the Secretary of State issuing an Order that the company or companies change their policy in a particular respect, although this is not usually necessary as the companies normally comply voluntarily with any recommendations that have been made. The DGFT has then the continuing responsibility to monitor these developments, but it is important to note that the MMC has no autonomous power of its own and cannot investigate or enforce its decisions itself. Only a relatively few monopoly references, between two and four, will be made every year, and many large companies with strong monopoly positions have never been investigated at all as they do not give cause for concern.

(b) Competition References. Because of the length of time that monopoly references take (and the consequent costs to the companies involved in providing information to the MMC), new legislation in the form of the Competition Act 1980 was introduced. This allows for a more selective investigation of any one practice carried out by a company, not necessarily a monopoly, that could be considered to be anti-competitive. This is defined as any course of conduct which restricts, distorts or prevents competition in the UK. Again it is the DGFT who has the responsibility for originally identifying such a practice, and he does a preliminary investigation to determine if it is truly anti-competitive. At the end of this, if the company concerned is prepared to abandon the practice, the matter goes no further, but if this is not acceptable a competition reference is made to the MMC which must decide not only whether the practice is anti-competitive but also whether it acts against the public interest. This investigation should be complete within six months, and again the Secretary of State has the power to enforce the finding of the MMC, should it go against the company. It is felt that in future far more use will be made of this procedure than the more unwieldy monopoly reference, particularly as both private and public corporations are subject to investigation. It has already been used to ensure that goods are not withheld from discount retail outlets, and against refusal to supply businesses which also deal with competitors.

(c) Mergers. The MMC has a further function that is suggested by its name–to consider certain mergers. Again, only a tiny minority of mergers are subject to investigation, as on the whole they are encouraged in the interests of creating efficient economic units. Occasionally however, it is considered necessary to consider the likely consequences of the takeover or merger of two or more businesses in the light of the public interest. The only mergers which are subject to examination are those which create or strengthen a monopoly (i.e. 25% of the market) and/or involve taking over assets in excess of £30 million. Thus both vertical and

horizontal mergers are covered, but only approximately 3% of all mergers are actually referred each year.

The decision to refer a merger is made by the Secretary of State based on advice from a non-statutory body headed by the DGFT. While under investigation, the merger can be suspended, although many will be dropped as a result of the decision to refer. The MMC are required to reach their conclusion within six months as to whether the merger will operate against the public interest, although they often do this within four. From the point of view of the companies involved, the quicker the report can be made the better as market conditions can change dramatically. Approximately 50% of those mergers which are referred will be found to be potentially harmful, and can then be forbidden to proceed by the Secretary of State if need be. Sometimes a reference is welcomed by the directors of a company if the bid was unwelcome.

The main criticism of this legislation is that the concept of the public interest which is laid down in the Fair Trading Act (and is all the MMC has to guide it when dealing with all three types of reference in this Section) is rather vague and it is difficult to know when or if a reference will be made. The MMC is often criticised for inconsistency for this reason, but this is rather unfair for, as already mentioned, it has no power to decide on references nor carry out its recommendations. The OFT is willing to advise companies contemplating a merger as to the likelihood of the proposed merger being referred. For this reason many qualifying mergers are brought to the attention of the DGFT although there is no duty to inform anyone. It is likely that a thorough overhaul of this area of law will take place in the near future, with changes suggested that may require companies to show positive benefits from a merger before it may proceed, rather than simply an absence of harm.

8.8   Restrictive Practices

In the area of restrictive practices the legislation is more positive. The Restrictive Trade Practices Act 1976 declares that restrictive practices are assumed to operate against the public interest unless they can be shown to do otherwise. Restrictive practices involve groups of apparently independent companies acting together, in what are often referred to as cartels, and making agreements which restrict their freedom to compete against one another in order to protect themselves. Probably the most common restrictive practice is price fixing, but market sharing, when the market is divided up into virtual monopolies, and collusive tendering are also frequent.

These practices have been tackled by requiring that all such agreements be made public on a register administered by the DGFT. When this requirement was originally introduced in 1956 many agreements were voluntarily dropped to avoid the publicity. Those that remain are eventually brought by the DGFT in front of the Restrictive Practices Court where the parties to the agreement must justify it on one of nine specific grounds, known as gateways, in order to continue to enforce it. The gateways include such matters as depriving the public of specific and substantial benefits, or preventing unemployment in an area of the country. It also has to be shown that on balance the restriction is not unreasonable, bearing in mind the interests of the parties and the public. Should this not prove possible, the Court declares the agreement to be void, and it therefore cannot be legally enforced. Once such a court order has been made, the continued enforcement of the agreement or indeed one of 'like effect' could render the parties liable to a fine. However, no penalty is possible before such a declaration has been made.

Very few agreements have managed to be justified, and few now are attempted, so that officially at least restrictive agreements are very rare. However, there is no penalty for not registering the agreement in the first place and every year the DGFT brings to light several agreements which are operating unlawfully. It is therefore difficult to judge whether the legislation has served to rid the economy of harmful restrictive practices or simply sent the remaining ones underground where it is more difficult for competitors to counter them.

Again the OFT is available to advise companies on how to draw up beneficial agreements in a way that either avoids the necessity to register or in which the restrictions are considered to be sufficiently insignificant to avoid the necessity of a court appearance after registration. Codes of practice tend to fall into this latter category, although they must be registered.

Another restrictive practice which is, however, dealt with under separate legislation is resale price maintenance (rpm). This too is in theory justifiable in front of the Restrictive Practices Court under the Resale Prices Act 1976, but in practice both individual and collective enforcement of rpm is banned as only two commodities, books and drugs, have gained exemption.

Recommended prices are allowed, however, but are subject to registration and further control (see further Section 9.5).

It can be seen that UK competition policy is somewhat *ad hoc* in its approach, with an administrative, investigative body dealing with monopoly power and a judicial body for considering restrictive practices which in reality are all part of the same problem. The importance of the rôle of the DGFT as a unifying influence can therefore be appreciated. The OFT, apart from the advice it will give to individual companies, also publishes useful explanatory literature.

8.9   EEC Competition Law

Mention must briefly be made of EEC competition law which will apply to any business whose activities are significant enough to affect trade within the Common Market. This does not necessarily mean that the company must be operating abroad within the EEC if it is so powerful in the UK that it effectively ties up the entire domestic market.

Competition policy is a fundamental part of the EEC's mission to create a free market throughout the member states and it is very vigorously pursued by the EEC Commission, the administrative body of the EEC. Unlike our domestic competition bodies, the Commission can initiate its own enquiries on the basis of its own observations or the complaints of competitors or customers, and it has wide powers to demand the production of documents and other evidence.

The law is found in Articles 85 and 86 of the Treaty of Rome and broadly prevents 'arrangements and concerted practices' (i.e. restrictive practices) which interfere with competition or 'abuse of a dominant position' (i.e. monopoly power) respectively. None of these terms is as clearly or precisely defined as UK law, but a company that is found to be breaching the Articles can be retrospectively fined up to 10% of its previous year's turnover. It is therefore vital that a company of any size takes specialist advice in this area, and also bears in mind 'anti-trust' legislation in the USA when trading there, as this is even more strictly applied and punitive in nature.

It is worth noting that the Commission is available to give 'negative clearance' to any practice which at first glance does not contravene the Articles, and although this is not binding it would mitigate any future fine. In addition, Article 85 allows for the exemption of certain practices which can be shown to be beneficial, but application must be made for this in advance and cannot be used as a defence once the practice has been uncovered. There is no equivalent exemption for Article 86.

Both Articles, in contrast to our domestic legislation, can be relied on as the basis of an action or as a defence in the English courts, and damages may be awarded as a result.

Questions

1 Account for the rise of the consumer protection movement. What are the aims of the movement and to what extent do you think they have been achieved?

2 Do you think it would be a good idea if all businesses were under a legal duty to trade fairly? What difficulties might there be in enforcing such a law?

3 Explain the role played by the following in consumer protection and/or competition policy:
   (a) the Director General of Fair Trading
   (b) the Monopolies and Mergers Commission
   (c) the Consumer Protection Advisory Committee
   (d) the Restrictive Practices Court
   (e) the Secretary of State for Trade and Industry
   (f) the EEC Commission
   (g) the Office of Fair Trading.

4 What are the advantages and disadvantages to:
   (a) businesses
   (b) consumers
   of relying on Codes of Practice to regulate business behaviour? Collect as much information as you can about various codes (available from your local Citizens Advice Bureau or the OFT) and assess how useful they are.

Chapter 9
Legal Control of Marketing Methods

Sophisticated marketing techniques have been a feature of business life since the consumer boom of the 1950s and 60s which in turn spawned the consumer movement, as shown in the previous chapter. It is not surprising therefore that some legislative control of these methods has been introduced to try to ensure that the legitimate aim of promoting the benefits of the product can be achieved without misleading, confusing or, in the extreme, deceiving the customer and without harming the interests of competitors. However, there is relatively little legislation in this area, which is partly a result of the success of the self-regulatory system which will be referred to later (see Section 9.4). This chapter will examine the most important of the controls which do exist to regulate promotional techniques.

9.1 Advertising and the Civil Law

Advertising is probably the most utilised and well known form of marketing and has existed in some form since Roman times. With the advent of the mass media, however, it has become ever more widespread. It was recognised by the Molony Committee and others that power wielded by the advertising agencies could be harmful if not checked. In theory, some methods of control existed in the civil law but were generally considered inadequate to protect consumers because of two major factors, one legal and one practical.

The first was the requirement in contract law for privity of contract which restricts the right to sue for broken promises in the agreement to the parties of that agreement. This means that in the case of a breach of contract, or even a misrepresentation which induces a party to enter a contract, only the seller of the product could be sued, and this is rarely the party who has made the promise in the first place, that is, the advertiser or manufacturer. Although compensation may be forthcoming from the retailer if an implied term had been broken (see Section 5.3), this did not put an advertiser under direct threat of being taken to court.

The second factor which 'shields' the advertiser from the bad publicity of a civil action is the practical point that each individual consumer who has been misled by an advertisement may not ever fully appreciate the extent of their misconceptions. In any case the consumer is likely to suffer a relatively small loss and therefore not be prepared to take lengthy and costly proceedings. Overall, however, the advertiser may be making substantial gains from such unscrupulous methods.

Consumers may not be the only parties hurt by unfair advertising. Competitors may also be undermined if their products are denigrated or successful marketing ploys copied too closely so that products become confused. In the first case, it would be possible for a company to sue another for 'slander of goods', a branch of the tort of *defamation*, if advertising claims slipped from fair comparison to untruthful slurs. Such 'comparative advertising' was until recently fairly rare in this country, and although it has now become more common there have been few cases in this area and this may explain why we, unlike most other countries, do not ban such comparisons outright. It would be left to a business to take action on its own behalf and show that the claims made were wholly false to maintain an action for slander of goods. Such civil action could of course take many months to complete by which time much damage could already have been done.

It is also possible for a business to sue for the tort of 'passing off'. This involves a competitor trying to make their product appear like that of another to cash in on that product's success. Again, however, such actions are comparatively unusual as it is difficult to satisfy the courts that what is being complained about is not just healthy competitiveness.

It was therefore considered that criminal controls were necessary in the interests of both competitors and customers. Although control over specific areas of advertising had existed earlier in the twentieth century, for example prohibiting advertising cures for cancer and VD, the Trade Descriptions Act 1968 was the first attempt to deal with the overall control of the content of advertising in general. It is worth noting that as yet there has been little attempt to control the amount or quality of advertising which the average person is exposed to every day. On occasion the MMC has drawn attention, but without major impact, to the difficulties for new competitors entering a market place where advertising expenditure is very high, for example in the detergent business.

9.2   The Trade Descriptions Act 1968

The 1968 Act deals with three specific types of claim which may be made by promoters of goods and services—claims about the physical characteristics and history of goods, false statements relating to the provision of services, and incorrect pricing of goods. The last aspect will be dealt with in the fuller discussion of control of pricing in Section 9.5.

(a) Section 1 of the Act makes it a criminal offence (punishable by a fine and/or imprisonment) to apply a false trade description or to offer to supply goods to which a false description has been applied. Section 2 lays down an exhaustive list of ten matters which constitute a trade description. These include statements relating to the physical characteristics and the history of the goods, including its quantity, size, method of manufacture, fitness for purpose, testing by any person, person by whom manufactured, and previous ownership or use. Anything else which does not come within section 2 cannot be a trade description and therefore, however false it may be, it will not constitute an offence. Examples which will fall outside the Act are so-called 'bait advertising' where goods are advertised on attractive terms but are then not available when customers turn up to buy them, and the contents of books and records are not clearly within section 2.

To be false the description must be false to a material degree or sufficiently misleading as to amount to the same thing. A trade description can be applied in the obvious way through being attached to the goods, or may be part of the packaging or display material used with the goods, or may be an oral statement made by a salesperson. Descriptions in advertisements for goods are to be taken to apply to all goods of the same type.

It is important to note that these provisions relate to goods only, and only when they are sold in the course of a trade or business, so private sellers are not subject to the Act. The offence is one of 'strict liability' which means that no deception or knowledge of the falsity of the description need be proved. If the description is false, the supplier of the goods and the applier of the description are guilty of an offence if they are acting in a business capacity.

However, a defence is open to those who unwittingly commit an offence by virtue of section 24 of the Act. This requires defendants to prove that the offence was committed through their own mistake, or in reliance on information provided, or was due to the act or default of another person and that the defendants took all reasonable precautions and exercised all due diligence to avoid the commission of the offence.

The extent of this defence was shown to be very wide in the case of *Tesco Supermarkets* v *Nattrass* [1972] A.C. 153. Tescos were prosecuted for allowing goods to be advertised as being available at a lower price than that at which they were sold, an offence under section 11 of the Act for which the section 24 defence is also available. Tesco's defence was that their store manager was at fault as he had put packets of washing powder at full price out for sale when they were advertised as being at cut price. Their contention was therefore that the store manager was 'another person' for the purposes of the Act, not to be associated with the company. By providing sufficient training and supervision of their staff the company had taken all reasonable precautions and exercised due diligence. This was accepted by the court and therefore Tescos were acquitted. The result of this decision is that unless it can be shown that someone high in the company's hierarchy, part of 'the directing mind and will of the organisation' such as a sales manager or possibly sales director or similar, is responsible for the false description, or that the supervision and training of other staff is insufficient, it will not be possible to hold large companies responsible for their false advertising claims. This therefore has led to a lack of prosecutions under the Act against advertising, and in fact the majority of prosecutions each year under section 1 are against car dealers for false odometer readings. However, the effectiveness of the Act as a general deterrent against unsubstantiated claims cannot be accurately assessed. The requirement to avoid applying a description to goods which can be said to be false to a material degree or grossly misleading is no doubt in the subconscious minds of most advertising executives when they prepare advertising copy.

(b) Section 14 of the Act makes it an offence to make a false statement about certain specified aspects of the provision of services. This, however, is not a strict liability offence and the prosecution must show that the statement was made knowing it to be false, or reckless as to whether it is true or false. Recklessness has been held to mean not paying sufficient attention to the truth or falsity of the statement, and does not require the statement maker to have reason to believe it was false.

In order for someone to be found guilty of an offence under section 14 it is necessary to show two things:

 (i) that the statement was false at the time it was made and
 (ii) that the party making it knew it was false at the time or paid insufficient regard to whether it was true or false.

Several cases involving travel companies have been successfully defended because it has been argued that statements made in brochures are simply predictions or referring to things which have not yet occurred and therefore cannot be either true or false when made. However, in *R.* v *Clarksons Holidays Limited* 116 S.J. 728 the company were found guilty for including an artist's impression of a completed hotel when it was clear that there was little chance of it being in that state when holidaymakers arrived, which proved substantially to be the case. Here the court held that the statement was untrue when it was made. It has also been held that if statements such as 'double rooms with balconies will be provided' were true when made as such rooms were available, the fact that the company negligently failed to ensure that customers got these rooms did not make the original statement 'reckless'.

The House of Lords recently decided in the case of *Wings Limited* v *Ellis* [1985] A.C. 272 that a travel company were guilty of making a false statement which they knew to be untrue even though at the time of the offence they had taken steps to correct their brochures. Someone, however, read an uncorrected version and a prosecution was brought. Their lordships pointed out that the offence was making a false statement which was known to be false, not knowingly making a false statement, so the fact that they were not aware that they were still making the statement was irrelevant. The company here could probably have relied on a section 24 defence, but this had been thought previously not to be available for section 14 offences and therefore the company was convicted. This case illustrates the very strict way in which judges interpret the words of statute, especially if they impose criminal penalties, and illustrates why careful statutory draftsmanship is so important.

9.3   Other Statutory Controls of Advertising

More specific controls of certain types of advertising also exist, and in fact over fifty Acts of Parliament deal in some way with aspects of advertising, although not exclusively. The best examples probably involve medicine, food and consumer credit, the last of which will be dealt with in Section 11.7 *(a)*. The Medicines Act 1968 prevents the advertising of drugs available only on prescription to the general public, and controls what must be included in advertising to doctors. Regulations made under the Food and Drugs legislation restrict what can be said in advertising for so-called 'diet foods' for example, and require the contents be listed in order of quantity on all foods. Where advertising can be sited is also controlled to a certain extent by the Town and Country Planning Acts, so that permission is needed to erect billboards and hoardings. The fact that more comprehensive legislation does not exist, however, is due largely to the success of the advertising industry in convincing governments that it can effectively and efficiently regulate itself.

9.4 The ASA and IBA

The Advertising Standards Authority (ASA) exists to influence the content of all advertisements except those on television and commercial radio, which are the responsibility of the Independent Broadcasting Authority (IBA). The ASA is an independent body which, though sponsored by the advertising industry, is not controlled by it. It performs its task by administering the British Code of Advertising Practice which lays down for advertisers a set of guidelines, summed up in its own advertising slogan that advertising should be 'Legal, Decent, Honest and Truthful'. The ASA investigates complaints from members of the public or others who feel that advertisements offend the code. If it upholds the complaint it will take steps to ensure that the advertisment is withdrawn. It has no statutory powers to do so, but acts through persuasion and the threat of withdrawal of media availability if need be. The ASA can be consulted by advertisers in advance if there are any doubts about the suitability of a campaign, which could save considerable sums of money being wasted.

The advertising industry maintains that it is a far better system than expensive and rigid legislative control. Some doubts have been expressed, however, as to whether the ASA is prepared to tackle more controversial subjects such as sexism and the promotion of materialism in advertising, though it must be said that at present the law is also unprepared to tackle these.

The IBA in contrast is a statutory body with the task of administering commercial television and radio programmes in general, including the content of advertising. They operate a similar code to the ASA, but with the important difference that all advertisements are vetted before they are allowed to be broadcast to ensure that they are acceptable. The Broadcasting Act 1981 itself also makes certain requirements, for example, no political or religious advertising is allowed, and there must be a perceivable break between advertisements and programmes.

As a result of an EEC directive, regulations are to be introduced that will allow the Director General of Fair Trading to apply for an injunction to prevent or ban misleading advertisements in circumstances where the voluntary controls are insufficient. This is the first example of legislative backing being given to voluntary codes and may be a pointer for future developments in the area of consumer protection. See further Sections 1.5 and 8.5.

9.5   Control of Pricing

Although methods of pricing can be seen as a form of advertising, it is considered separately here. It has been dealt with by the legislature as a separate issue in recent years because it has become apparent that pricing claims have been used as a major, though often misleading, incentive to buy.

Pricing policy is very much for the individual business to decide on for itself. Contrary to popular belief, there is no 'right' price for goods or services as the price is whatever the market will bear. Since the original Resale Prices Act was passed in 1964, resale price maintenance has been effectively abolished except for two commodities, books and drugs. This means that manufacturers cannot impose a price on retailers at which they must sell goods. The retailer may decide to sell at the recommended price, but cannot be compelled to do so by, for example, a threat by the manufacturer to withdraw supplies. (An exception to this rule is where goods are sold as 'loss leaders', when suppliers may take action to protect themselves). There is also no requirement to display prices on goods or services but if it is done the information must be accurate and conveyed in a particular manner, otherwise an offence under the Trade Descriptions Act, section 11, or the Price Marking (Bargain Offers) Order 1978 may have been committed.

(a) Section 11 of the Act

This makes three requirements:

(i) Where prices for goods are compared with the recommended price, these must be the generally accepted manufacturers' recommended prices for that area. This provision is held by many to be responsible for the practice of 'sky pricing' whereby recommended prices are set at unrealistically high levels so that apparently large discounts can be made. Further action was therefore taken to control this, see *(b)* below.

(ii) Where prices are reduced they must have been sold at the higher price for at least twenty-eight consecutive days in the last six months. This is to prevent Sale prices which are no cheaper than previous prices, or higher prices that have only been charged for a very short time being reduced. It is also designed to prevent 'stale' reductions where goods have been at the lower price for a considerable period. Because there is no such thing as the correct price for goods, such prices are in reality the going rate rather than a reduction, but customers can be misled into being less discerning if they believe they are getting a bargain. Nevertheless, the Act specifically allows for disclaimers (such as 'reduced prices have not necessarily been charged for twenty-eight days in the last six months'), which most stores now use automatically in Sales to avoid inadvertently committing an offence. Also there is no requirement that the previous price should have been charged in the same premises and can therefore be that charged in quite another part of the country. These limitations on this provision have rendered it virtually useless to achieve its original purposes.

(iii) Goods must not be offered for sale at a price lower than that at which they are actually available. Thus in the case of goods which have been mistakenly underpriced, an offence will have been committed under the Act, although of course there is no requirement to sell at the lower price as only an invitation to treat has been made. See Section 4.3 *(a)*.

As with all criminal law, even when an offence has been committed, there will not automatically be a prosecution. This may simply be because the crime is undetected, but may also be due to the fact that the enforcing agency, in this case local Trading

Standards Officers, may prefer to warn the traders rather than take full proceedings in an attempt to educate them to maintain higher standards.

It is important to note that section 11 only relates to mispricing of goods, and so, as no mention of price is made in section 14 of the Act, no offence will be committed when false claims are made about the price of services. This has led courts to decide on several occasions that claims relating to sales and refunds of prices are not covered by any aspect of the legislation. For instance, proven untrue claims that a store is closing down, or that money will be refunded if lower prices are found elsewhere are outside the provisions of the Act and therefore no offence has been committed. It would also appear that claims that goods are given 'free' when in fact the cost of them is recouped by increasing the price of the accompanying product may also be outside the scope of the Act.

(b) Price Marking (Bargain Offers) Order

This Order was an attempt to ban misleading price comparisons by requiring them to be phrased in a particular way. Clearly prohibited are vague statements such as 'Worth £50, Our Price £40', although this would be legitimate if the source of the £50 price were identified. However, the legislation is complex and badly drafted and is due to be amended in the near future. It does illustrate a problem encountered by the legislature in this area in that the control of certain practices simply leads to the development of more misleading, but legitimate, practices being invented, such as the appearance of the ubiquitous and meaningless 'after sale price'.

The Order also bans quoting of recommended prices on furniture and domestic electric and gas appliances, because they tended to bear no relation to prices actually being charged. It has been suggested that all recommended prices be banned and this may be introduced in the amending legislation.

9.6   Pyramid Selling

Pyramid selling is a form of selling which primarily involves selling the marketing technique rather than a product. It acquired its name as it depends on an increasingly large number of suppliers becoming involved in the process. Typically it involves a promoter who begins the business by involving several others to sell the product, usually among their friends, neighbours and colleagues.

They then make a profit not only on the goods they sell but also on introducing new sellers into the pyramid. The problem is that an increasing number of people are attempting to sell what are often highly priced products of doubtful usefulness in an increasingly small market. This practice was becoming widespread towards the end of the 1960s and many people were losing money after paying to enter such schemes and finding themselves unable to dispose of the product. Provisions were therefore included in the Fair Trading Act 1973 for regulations to be made which have served to control this procedure, although not to ban it entirely.

The Act makes it a criminal offence to accept money or to induce others to pay money in return for the prospect of earning money themselves in the future by introducing new participants into such a trading scheme. Bonuses can therefore only be earned in direct relation to the amount of the product that is sold by participants and by those they have introduced. Regulations require that a limit be placed on the amount of money which can be charged to enter a scheme (currently £25) and allow people a 'cooling-off period' in which to change their minds about participating in the scheme. This is to try to deter over-enthusiastic selling of the scheme by those depending on further participants for their income. Persons who wish to enter must be given a specified amount of information in writing about the scheme and, if and when they choose to leave, they are guaranteed the right to sell back any products which they cannot dispose of at not less than 90% of the purchase price less any deterioration. Although several such schemes continue to operate in this country, they now have to do so within these constraints.

9.7   Inertia Selling

The success of inertia selling as a promotion method rests on people's basic idleness and lack of legal knowledge. It involves sending entirely unsolicited and, usually, expensive products to unsuspecting people and informing them that although under no obligation to buy, if they do not wish to avail themself of the magnificent offer, they should return the goods within (say) thirty days. Often this was not done, out of forgetfulness, and after thirty-one days a bill would be delivered to the now exasperated customer which he or she felt obliged to pay. Had such persons known of the case of *Felthouse* v *Bindley* (see Section 4.6) they would have been aware that they had not accepted the offer made to them and were therefore under no obligation to pay up.

Following complaints about this technique, the Unsolicited Goods and Services Act 1971 was passed which gives customers extra rights. These are that the goods become an unconditional gift to the recipient if nothing is done for six months. This period is shortened to thirty days if the recipient writes stating that the product is unwanted and is available for collection. In addition it was made a criminal offence to demand payment or take steps to procure payment such as threatening legal action when goods or services had been supplied unsolicited. This last provision has meant that the practice has more or less died out.

It should be noted that sending unsolicited goods is not in itself an offence. An exception, totally prohibited by this legislation, is sending unsolicited books, magazines, etc. which portray human sexual techniques.

9.8 Doorstep Selling

The door-to-door selling of goods and services causes concern because such traders often use over-persuasive selling techniques on people who have not sought out their wares in the first place, and may be in a vulnerable position. Also such traders are not constrained by the need to build up and maintain a good local business reputation in the same way as more static forms of business. The EEC has suggested that all such traders should be controlled, but so far only door-to-door peddlers of goods and services on credit have been regulated in the UK. See Section 11.7 (*a*). The OFT has recently been concerned about the increased use of the telephone to make unsolicited sales overtures, but so far has attempted to curb this through self-regulatory techniques rather than the introduction of new legislation.

Questions

1 Do you consider that it is necessary to control advertising by legislation? Take time to examine examples of everyday advertisements thoroughly before answering this question.

2 Evaluate the role of the ASA in controlling advertising. They can be contacted to provide information on their activities at the following address:

> ASA Limited, Department C, Brook House,
> Torrington Place, London WC1E 7HN.

3 Why was the *Tesco* v *Nattrass* case important in determining the scope of the Trade Descriptions Act?

4 To what extent and with what success has the legislature attempted to control the following undesirable selling techniques?

> Inertia Selling
> Pyramid Selling
> False Bargain Offers
> Doorstep Selling

5 From your own experience can you think of any other form of marketing which requires an element of legal control in the interests of both customers and competitors? How would you draft such a law and what problems might it cause?

6 Jane and John book a holiday with Swingles Ltd. The brochure describes their hotel as 'overlooking the sandy beach' and that in addition a swimming pool is available for clients' use. When they arrive at the resort, they discover that the hotel overlooks the coach station, the beach is made up of stones and shingle, and the swimming pool is empty. Have Swingles Ltd. committed any criminal offences? What would you advise Jane and John to do?

Chapter 10

Safety

An important consideration for releasing goods and services on to the market should obviously be whether they can be utilised safely, and for this purpose testing and trials will be undertaken. This chapter considers what standards the law requires and how far legal liability may be incurred if it transpires that the products cause damage or injury to users.

10.1 Product Liability

The term 'product liability' is a familiar one to American lawyers and is becoming increasingly so in the UK, although at present we have no specific branch of law dealing with the problem of who is liable to whom when a defective or dangerous product causes injury. Before the introduction of the EEC directive on product liability (see Section 10.4) the position in this country depended on general principles of contract and tort, which will be examined below.

It must be stressed that what is under consideration here is the civil law, which means in practice responsibility to pay compensation for injuries caused to persons or property. This would normally be covered by insurance policies, although product liability insurance is not compulsory and the level required by a particular business would need to be assessed in the light of the possible extent of liability outlined here.

10.2 The Contractual Position

As has already been explained, when goods are supplied they must be as described, of merchantable quality and fit for a particular purpose made known, regardless of which type of contract the goods are supplied under. A contract purely for services must be performed with reasonable care and skill. In contracts for goods made with a consumer, these terms can never be excluded, but between businesses a valid exclusion clause could be used if it satisfies the reasonableness test. (See further Sections 5.4 and 6.4). Liability in these cases is strict, which means that it does not require a finding of fault for the seller to be responsible for the breach. This was well illustrated in the case of *Frost* v *Aylesbury Dairy Company* [1905] 1 K.B. 608 where the dairy was liable for the germs in their milk although there was no way they could have detected or eliminated them. The milk was not fit for its purpose, drinking, and therefore they were in breach of contract and thereby liable for the illness of the consumer.

Thus a business would be liable to the party to whom the goods were sold for any breach of the contractual implied terms, provided they had not been effectively excluded. This liability would extend back up the chain of contracts between retailer, wholesaler, distributor and manufacturer, etc. But the limitations of this liability are as follows:

(a) The concept of merchantability, etc. only applies when the goods are first sold and does not necessarily require them to be reasonably safe, only reasonably fit for their purpose. Therefore if there is a lapse of time before damage occurs it is always open to argument that the goods were merchantable when sold and that the defect was due to wrongful use, storage or some other matter.

(b) Because of the privity of contract rule the only person who has a contractual claim is the actual buyer, or his/her principal if the buyer bought as agent (see Chapter 7). Anybody else who suffered loss or injury as a result of the defect–a passerby, friend or member of the buyer's household–would have no claim in contract at all. Neither could the actual buyer claim compensation on behalf of someone else, as he or she can only claim for personal losses.

10.3 Tort Liability

Injured persons who did not happen to have acquired the goods which injured them would have to rely on a less straightforward claim in negligence. The tort or civil wrong of negligence applies in many different circumstances, but its modern development owes much to a case involving product liability. In *Donoghue* v *Stevenson* [1932] A.C. 562 Mrs. Donoghue visited a café and her friend ordered two glasses of ginger beer. Mrs. Donoghue drank some of the liquid straight from the opaque bottle and then poured the remainder over her ice cream. To her horror out came the decomposing remains of a snail. As a consequence Mrs. Donoghue was ill and wished to claim compensation but as her friend had made the contract with the retailer, she had to take another action. She, or rather her legal adviser, chose the then novel course of suing the manufacturer in tort. This required there to be a finding that:

(a) The defendant (i.e. in this case the manufacturer) owed a duty of care to the plaintiff (in this case Mrs. Donoghue). The law does not require everyone to take care for everyone else, only those whom they could 'reasonably foresee' they would harm if they did not take care. In the course of the decision, Lord Atkin expressed this duty in terms of taking care for one's neighbour and the House of Lords decided that Mrs. Donoghue and the manufacturer Stevenson were sufficiently close to one another for such a duty to exist.

(b) The defendant breached the standard of care required. This forms the essence of many claims of negligence in practice – did the defendant do less than the law requires? The standard used is that of the 'reasonable man' in the circumstances of the case. In *Donoghue* v *Stevenson* it was the standard of the reasonable manufacturer – not Stevenson's own standards, or those of a mythical perfect manufacturer of ginger beer, but a reasonable one. Evidence of what is standard practice in the trade would obviously be important here but as the court applies an objective test it may not necessarily regard the 'average' as the same as the 'reasonable'.

(c) The damage was caused as a direct consequence of the negligent action. Again a test of reasonable foreseeability is applied here – could the type of damage actually caused have been foreseen? If the answer is yes, then the defendant is liable for all losses, even if the scale is far higher than could be foreseen, but if the answer is no, the defendant is not liable at all.

The decision in the case of *Donoghue* v *Stevenson* that Stevenson owed a duty of care to Mrs. Donoghue means that it is well established that manufacturers can be found liable for injury caused to the ultimate consumer. However, it must be stressed that this is by no means automatic as the following illustrations show. It may be difficult for the injured party to identify who was at fault, i.e. who of those in the manufacturing chain fell below the reasonable standard of care and therefore was negligent. Unlike in a contractual claim, it is not automatically clear whom to sue as, for instance, the retailer, wholesaler, designer, manufacturer or component manufacturer may be the party who was at fault. It may be particularly difficult to identify the transgressor if the defective product involved is a complicated design and may be totally altered or destroyed by the incident which caused the injuries. Once having identified who was most likely to have been at fault, the plaintiff still has to gather sufficient, often technical, evidence to show that the standard of care was not reached, and this only has to be that of a reasonable man. After five years and extensive research the lawyers advising the parents of children who were born deformed as a result of the use of the thalidomide drug in the 1960s, could not be certain that they could prove that Distillers Company Ltd. had done less than reasonable drug manufacturers at the time should have done to test a product, even though there was no doubt that the drug had caused the harm. Ultimately also the plaintiff may be held to be partly to blame for the accident, and damages are reduced accordingly for this contributory negligence.

In practice these difficulties have meant that injured parties, particularly if they are individuals having to rely on Legal Aid to pursue their case, have often dropped their claims or settled out of court for small sums offered as *ex gratia* payments by manufacturers because of the uncertainty in pursuing such a case. Consumer groups, and the Royal Commission set up after the thalidomide disaster, have drawn attention to the unsatisfactory state of the law in this area for many years, but reform is now imminent as a result of the adoption by the EEC of a directive on product liability. (For the position if the defective product had been bought using credit facilities, see Section 11.7).

10.4   The EEC Product Liability Directive

This directive was finally adopted in July 1985 after nearly ten years' debate. New laws have to be introduced in all the member states, including the UK, to comply with its provisions by July 1988. Although the exact details of the law in Britain have yet to be announced, some indication can be given of the likely format which will involve an additional right of action against businesses whose products prove to be defective.

The fundamental change that will be made is that producers of defective goods will be strictly liable to the injured user for both personal injury and damage to private property. This would mean that anyone, regardless of whether he or she is the buyer of the defective product, will be able to look to the producer for compensation without having to show that it was the producer's fault through lack of reasonable care. However, compensation will still not be automatic every time anyone is injured as a result of using a product. The injured party will still have to prove the product was defective and that it was the defect which caused the injury. This is known as the 'causal relationship'. Producers will also be able to use as a defence the fact that a product was not defective at the time it left their control.

For the purposes of this new law when it is introduced, the term producer will include the manufacturer, component-part manufacturer, importer into the EEC, anyone who puts his trade name on the product and any supplier who fails to identify who the producer is. Any of these may be jointly liable, and the definition is aimed to ensure that the injured party can find someone to hold responsible. A product will be 'defective' if it does not provide the safety which a party is entitled to expect, bearing in mind such matters as warnings and instructions given with the product, the use to which it could reasonably be expected to be put and the time it was marketed. This obviously goes further than our own concept of fitness for purpose. Liability will remain for ten years after the product was first put into circulation and the legislation will not be retrospective.

After much controversy member states are to be allowed to introduce a 'development risk defence' into their legislation and it would seem that this will be included in UK legislation. This would mean that a producer would be able to claim that at the time the product was put on the market the state of scientific or technological knowledge was not such as to enable the existence of the defect to be discovered, i.e. that the defect was undetectable. This is likely to be of most use in the pharmaceutical and high-tech industries where new complicated products are being introduced, and a large burden would be thrown back on the injured party to prove the defect was detectable. It should be noted that this defence will not be available in all member states to which a business may export its products. Although trade and industry have resisted this change in the law, it must be pointed out that strict liability is not a new concept and has existed since before the first Sale of Goods Act in 1893 for sellers of goods.

Obviously before the law is introduced, some time before July 1988, businesses will want to reassess their quality control methods and the warnings and instructions given with their products, as well as checking that their insurance cover is adequate to deal with any potential liability. Again there is no suggestion that such insurance cover will be compulsory.

10.5 Employers' Liability for Unsafe Tools and Equipment

Strict liability has also existed for some time in the workplace. The Employer's Liability (Defective Equipment) Act 1969 makes employers strictly liable for damage caused to their employees through using faulty products required at work. Thus the onus of finding whom to blame for the fault is placed on the employer, who is therefore under an extra legal duty to ensure that suppliers of equipment for use at work are trustworthy. See also the criminal controls against faulty goods being used at work, Section 10.8 below.

10.6 Criminal Control of Safety

In recent years criminal penalties have been introduced in an attempt to prevent unsafe goods getting on to the market in the first place, rather than strengthening the right to compensation, on the principle that 'prevention is better than cure'. However, there is as yet no comprehensive legal control of the safety standards of goods. Legislation may be introduced in the future, possibly at the same time as the EEC Product Liability directive is implemented, to require that all goods meet sound modern standards of safety, however this may be defined. For the moment, the legislation is somewhat piecemeal and no government agency is responsible for the testing of products before they are sold, or imported into this country.

10.7 Consumer Safety Act 1978

This legislation gives power to the Secretary of State for Trade and Industry to make regulations to ensure that goods are safe in respect of such matters as their design, or compliance with standards. Supplying goods in breach of .these regulations is a criminal offence punishable by a maximum fine of two thousand pounds and/or three months imprisonment. As yet only approximately twenty-five regulations have been made under this Act and its predecessors. Some regulations cover a wide range of products such as electrical equipment, others are very specialised, dealing with one particular type of product, for example the regulation which forbids the inclusion of a cord in children's anorak hoods. This means that a large number of products are entirely unregulated and there are some strange anomalies within the regulations: for instance, children's nightdresses have to be made of non-flammable material but children's pyjamas do not!

To deal with the problem of new dangerous products arriving on the market which are not covered by existing regulations, the Secretary of State has the power to issue prohibition orders and notices. The former place a ban on the supply of all products of the type dealt with in the Order for a period of twelve months, after which a regulation may be passed or the ban lapses. The latter require an individual named in the Order to cease supplying a particular product, and have not been widely used. The Secretary of State can also issue 'notices to warn' which require suppliers of unsafe goods to issue warning notices. However, there are no powers to order a compulsory recall of unsafe goods, the legislature appearing to rely on the goodwill of businesses to do this voluntarily when need be. Breach of any of these orders is likewise a criminal offence. This legislation is enforced by local Trading Standards departments, who have limited powers to enter and inspect premises and seize goods in pursuance of these duties.

The Consumer Safety (Amendment) Act 1986 gives Trading Standards Officers additional rights to detain imported goods for up to forty-eight hours in order to inspect them, but compensation will be payable to the owners if the goods are found to be satisfactory.

An additional provision of the Consumer Safety Act 1978 allows anyone injured as a result of the breach of any regulation or order to sue the supplier directly for 'breach of statutory duty', irrespective of any rights that party may have in contract or tort.

Many of the regulations that have been passed incorporate, or are based on, existing British Standards Institute standards, i.e. the government-sponsored agency which issues the Kite mark for displaying on goods which meet its requirements. Apart from in these circumstances, however, there is no obligation for goods to comply with BSI standards, although it is obviously a good marketing point if the Kite mark can be used.

10.8   The Health and Safety at Work Act

In one area, a general duty to ensure that goods are reasonably safe already exists, and that is when they are supplied for use at work. Section 6 of the Health and Safety at Work Act states that it is the duty of anyone who designs, manufactures, imports or supplies any article for use at work to ensure, so far as is reasonably practicable, that the article is so designed and constructed as to be safe and without risk to health when properly used. It is a criminal offence punishable by a fine or imprisonment not to comply. It might be questioned why individuals should be better protected against injury in their workplace, and more onerous responsibilities be placed on those supplying products which happen to be used at work, both in criminal and civil law, than elsewhere.

10.9   Other Criminal Statutory Control of Safety

The Medicines Act 1968 was introduced to strengthen the control of the drugs available in this country in the wake of the thalidomide tragedy. In order to supply medicines, manufacturers have to satisfy the government body, the Committee on the Safety of Medicines, of various matters including that their premises and facilities are adequate to produce drugs, and that new products are safe and of a satisfactory quality and efficacy. It should be noted that the Committee itself does not do any testing of drugs, but relies on information, supplied by the manufacturers and feedback from doctors and others, to exercise its authority. The supply of poisons is controlled by separate legislation.

Motor cars are potentially very dangerous products, and are therefore fairly strictly controlled by regularly updated regulations made under the Road Traffic Acts, i.e. the Motor Vehicles (Construction and Use) Regulations. These cover such matters as the compulsory inclusion of front seat belts and other safety features. It is also a criminal offence to supply a car which is unroadworthy.

Food products must be fit for human consumption and of the nature, substance and quality demanded by the Food Act 1984. Regulations also require some information be given about the contents of food, including for instance the inclusion of additives and preservatives which are identified by E numbers in compliance with EEC rules, so that it is possible for sensitive people to avoid substances to which they are allergic. It is likely that more extensive labelling requirements will be introduced in the near future.

It would of course also be a criminal offence to describe falsely the safety attributes or fitness for purpose of a product under the Trade Description Act section 1, see Section 9.2.

Questions

1 What do you understand by the term product liability?
2 Give an account of the facts and decisions in the following cases:
   (a) *Frost* v *Aylesbury Dairies*
   (b) *Donoghue* v *Stevenson*
   and explain their importance in the area of product liability.
3 Outline the effect of the changes that introduction of the EEC directive on product liability will bring to businesses and to consumers. The law will be found in the Consumer Protection Act when passed by Parliament sometime in 1987 or 1988.
4 How far do you consider that the Consumer Safety Act meets its aim of ensuring 'prevention rather than cure'?
5 Explain how people at work are more protected against injury from unsafe products than elsewhere. Can you account for this difference?
6 Do you think there should be stricter safety regulations and checks in this country, for example at ports? Give reasons for your answers.
7 Your company manufactures electrical appliances which are sold to both other businesses and the general public. Over the last three months you have received complaints from five different buyers that one particular product, launched at the beginning of 1987, is faulty. One private purchaser, Mr. A. is threatening to sue both your company and the retailer from whom he purchased the appliance, as a result of injuries caused to his son when he used the appliance and suffered an electric shock and burns. He is claiming compensation of £5000.

   You are asked to submit a report detailing what your company's potential civil and criminal liability could be in these circumstances, and give advice as to the best course of action, bearing in mind both the legal position and business realities. Indicate how your advice would differ, if at all, if the EEC directive on product liability had been adopted.

Chapter 11
Methods of Payment and Finance

Goods and services once successfully produced, marketed and sold must be paid for. Much of how this is done is left to negotiation between the parties, but in areas where concern has been felt about possible exploitation, for example in the granting of credit to consumers, the legislature has stepped in to regulate the relationship. This chapter will examine the legal framework within which this most vital element in the business process is conducted.

11.1 Duty to Pay

As has already been noted, the level of prices for goods and services is purely a matter for negotiation between the parties, unless none has been agreed when a 'reasonable' price would be payable (see Sections 4.7(a), 5.2, 5.11 and 9.5). An invoice is simply a request for payment and has no legal significance. Anything written on the invoice probably does not form part of the contract as it has appeared too late in the exchange of documents (see Sections 4.7(b) and 6.2) and will not therefore be binding, but will be useful evidence of the terms previously agreed.

The Sale of Goods Act, section 28, stipulates that delivery of the goods and payment of the price are concurrent conditions, i.e. that delivery and payment should take place at the same time, and that once property in the goods has passed to the buyer an action for the price may be taken by the seller. However, this is subject to other agreement in the contract and in practice, apart from in retail sales, this would hardly ever apply, payment normally coming some time after delivery. See Section 11.4.

The debtor (i.e. the party owing money) is under a duty to seek out and pay the creditor at a reasonable time in legal tender, which consists of bank notes, 50p pieces totalling no more than £10, silver coins of 20p or less totalling no more than £5 and bronze coins up to 20p. The creditor is not obliged to accept anything else and can demand to be paid the amount exactly and not give any change. Most business accounts will not be paid in cash, however, but through cheques or other forms of money transfer. Again a creditor is not obliged to accept these methods of payment, although in practice these will usually be more convenient.

Any debtor who does not pay will be in breach of contract and can be sued for default. Payment may be withheld while any dispute about the quality or the fitness of goods or services is settled, which obviously puts the buyer in a stronger position to negotiate. However, care should be taken to make the basis of the withholding of payment clear, as interest may be payable on overdue sums if this has been included as a term in the contract and is not a penalty clause (see Section 6.6). Should the dispute reach court, the court may award interest on the claim even if it is paid before judgement, although not if it has been settled before proceedings start.

In order to obtain payment earlier than may otherwise be possible, businesses sometimes make use of factors who buy trade debts for their value less commission and then collect the debt later themselves. Notice of this must be given to the debtor in writing, and in practice this is usually done through stamping the invoice with the appropriate information.

Debts of a company which has gone into liquidation owing money will be paid out of the assets of the company. Secured creditors such as banks will be paid after other priority groups such as the Inland Revenue and the employees, and normal unsecured trade creditors will be paid last out of the residue, if any. In circumstances where liabilities exceed assets, as is common in a liquidation, unsecured creditors may get nothing or a small proportion of the payment due. This explains the popularity of Romalpa clauses in recent years (see Section 6.7) and the importance of taking such steps as are practicable to check the creditworthiness of those with whom business is done. With individuals this can be done through consulting credit reference agencies which keep a check on people's previous bad debts. With companies this can be done through formal channels such as checking the published accounts, the companies' registers of charges and debenture holders (see Section 11.8), taking up bank and other references or making use of specialised commercial agencies which provide information on the creditworthiness of companies.

11.2   Payment by Cheque

Cheques are a form of negotiable instrument, the term used to describe the process devised by traders whereby money value can be freely transferred without the necessity to carry and transfer large sums of cash. They are an example of a type of negotiable instrument known as bills of exchange which have to be drawn on (i.e. paid out by) a bank.

Banks and their customers have a contract between them under which the bank undertakes to honour cheques by the customer, provided the account is in credit or within an agreed overdraft. Banks also provide advice and other forms of money management in return for a fee, in the form of bank charges, and have the right to use the money deposited to earn interest. Banks, apart from the Bank of England, are commercial concerns and exist to earn profits for their shareholders in the same way as other companies. However, the ways in which they operate are controlled by legislation in the form of the Banking Act 1979, the Cheques Act 1957 and Common Law rules about negotiable instruments, the details of which are outside the scope of this book.

A bank which fails to pay out from an account which is in credit is liable for breach of contract to its customer. Conversely, if it pays to the wrong party, it cannot hold its customer liable and debit the account unless the customer had drawn the cheque negligently or if in some other way the bank is not at fault.

When cheques are 'crossed' this is an instruction to the bank only to pay out through another bank so the cheque cannot be simply cashed. Special crossings such as 'account payee only' give even more definite instructions to the bank, and prevent money being paid to the wrong party.

The obligation to pay a debt is not finally discharged until the cheque is honoured. When a cheque has been paid out, this is evidence that the payee has received the money and thus acts as a form of receipt.

11.3   Other Methods of Payment

Large sums of money which need to be paid immediately can be drawn on a bank in the form of a bank transfer or bankers' draft. International sales are often paid for by way of bills of exchange which is a method of ensuring that payment is made. The bill has to be paid by the buyer, usually three months after it is drawn up, but the advantage to the seller is that it can be discounted at an earlier date or used as security for an overdraft in the meantime. As bills of exchange are negotiable instruments they can be transferred from one party to another, usually at less than their full face value, until the final payment to whoever holds the bill at the payment date.

Extra protection when selling abroad can be gained through the government insurance scheme run by the Export Credits Guarantee Department.

11.4   Credit

Anything which is not paid for immediately – cash on delivery (COD) or in a simple retail transaction – has been bought on credit and many business deals are expressly or impliedly subject to one month for payment. More specifically, credit implies a formal arrangement whereby one party (the creditor) allows the other (the debtor) a facility to pay back money lent, or owed, over a period of time at a charge. Such facilities enable customers to buy more than they could afford to pay for at once and are therefore very valuable to business and attractive to customers. To avoid exploitation of this, however, Parliament has seen fit to control the activities of creditors in the interests of current and would-be debtors, particularly those without business experience. Any business which involves the granting or arranging of credit facilities to consumers and small businesses must be aware of the implications of the legislation.

11.5   The Consumer Credit Act 1974

This Act was passed to provide a comprehensive regulation of the granting of credit to consumers. It lays down a very detailed series of regulations of which only the main features can be dealt with here. Many of the provisions were not new and had applied previously, but only to certain types of credit such as hire-purchase and money lending. The difference is that the 1974 Act applies to all forms of credit provided for 'individuals', which for the purposes of this legislation covers everyone that is not a corporate body (i.e. a company) where the amount of credit supplied does not exceed £15 000. Thus both business partnerships and sole traders are protected along with 'ordinary' consumers.

The figure of £15 000 was updated from £5000 in May 1985 and will no doubt be increased again in the future. It is calculated by deducting from the total sum involved any deposit and other immediate costs plus the charge for credit, such as interest, etc. So a transaction involving the purchase of, say, a boat for £18 000 where £1000 was paid as deposit and the interest and other charges amounted to £2000 would still be within the Act. All agreements which fall within this category are regulated agreements and subject to the controls in the legislation, unless expressly exempted from it. The most important categories of transactions which are exempt are mortgages from building societies, local authorities and other bodies for the purchase of homes, low-cost straightforward money loans such as may be given by an employer to an employee for the purchase of a season ticket, and normal 'trade credit' where payment is made in four or fewer instalments. This last exemption means that it is unnecessary for every milkman and newsagent to be subject to the Act for allowing the milk or newspaper bill to accumulate to the end of the week.

The Act also covers consumer hire agreements which are capable of lasting for more than three months and do not involve total payments of more than £15 000. As the definition of 'individual' again includes sole traders and partners this may affect companies which lease business equipment to traders as well as, more obviously, television and car rental companies. For simplicity, credit agreements will be referred to throughout the following sections, although most of the provisions also apply to hire agreements.

11.6 Licensing of Creditors

The immediate requirement made by the Act is for all those businesses connected with consumer credit and hire to be licensed by the Director General of Fair Trading. These include what are referred to as ancillary credit businesses, such as credit brokers and debt collectors. Over 125 000 licences have been issued in all. In order to issue a licence, the DGFT must receive the completed application forms and appropriate fee and satisfy himself that the applicant is a 'fit person' to hold a licence. In determining this question the DGFT has a wide amount of discretion but can take into consideration such matters as accounts of previous trading malpractice, criminal offences by the company or individuals involved, or evidence of discrimination in their methods of granting credit.

To operate such a business without a licence is a criminal offence and, perhaps even more importantly, any agreements made by an unlicensed creditor will be unenforceable against the debtor unless the DGFT agrees otherwise. The licences are renewable every fifteen years, and can be suspended or withdrawn at any time during this period. This form of administrative control obviously acts as a strong incentive for creditors to ensure that their staff are well trained and aware of all the obligations placed on them by the Act.

11.7   Obligations of Licensed Creditors

(a) *Seeking business*

Such obligations include strict requirements about the form and content of advertisements for credit facilities which are laid down in regulations. Most credit advertisements must include the APR, an abbreviated form of the 'annual percentage rate of the true rate of interest' which must be calculated by a set, and very complicated, formula so that debtors have a way of comparing the different costs of the various forms of credit available. Other information must also be disclosed to the same end.

Restrictions are also placed on other methods of canvassing for business. No door-to-door selling of pure money loans is allowed unless a written request for this from the would-be debtor has been received. Door-to-door selling of credit facilities for specific goods or services, such as double glazing, is permitted if the creditor is specially licensed to do so. To deter over-enthusiastic selling of such facilities, debtors are allowed a 'cooling-off period' of approximately ten days during which time they may cancel agreements which have been preceded by oral negotiations (therefore excluding mail order), signed by them away from business premises associated with the creditor. Note that this exception to the rule that once a contract is made it binds the parties immediately only applies to credit, and then only when the agreement is signed off trade premises, usually at the consumer's home.

(b) *Documentation*

All credit agreements have to be in writing, and the form and content of these are carefully controlled by a series of regulations effective from 1985. In addition to including certain information, which sometimes has to be in a particular set form of words, they must be legible and signed by the debtor, otherwise they may be totally unenforceable. The courts, not the DGFT, have to be applied to in these circumstances. Creditors are also required to supply debtors with copies of agreements they have signed within a certain time, and again if these requirements are not met the agreement may be unenforceable. In practice this would mean the creditor would have no legal means of recovering either the goods or services provided, nor of suing the debtor for non-payment. It is therefore essential that creditors organise their paperwork efficiently.

(c) The cost of credit

Apart from the obligation to disclose the true cost of credit through the use of the APR, a check is also kept on the level of the cost of credit through allowing debtors to challenge an agreement they have entered into as 'extortionate' if, for instance, it involves paying an exorbitant rate of interest. This can be taken to court as a separate issue or raised by the debtor during other proceedings. The court may then totally change the amounts involved or even order the creditor to pay back sums already paid by the debtor if it agrees that the bargain was extortionate. This section of the Act is not subject to the £15 000 limit and applies only to consumer credit agreements, not hiring agreements.

(d) Other obligations

In order to ensure that creditors take some responsibility for the quality of the outlet through which their credit facilities are offered, the creditor is made jointly liable for defective goods or services provided by a supplier with whom the creditor has pre-existing arrangements, such as credit card companies or finance companies and retailers. This means that if the supplier has gone out of business or refuses to deal with the customer's complaint when goods or services costing more than £100 have been bought on credit, the customer could take action against the creditor for the whole of the amount lost, including damages for breach of contract.

This provision, found in section 75 of the Act, does not apply to HP agreements, because here the goods will have been sold to the creditor to supply to the consumer directly so that the creditor and the supplier are the same person. However, in order to protect the debtor, the negotiator of the deal, often a car dealer or other retailer, will be deemed to be acting as the agent of the creditor and therefore the creditor will be bound by anything said during the course of the negotiations.

Because of the special nature of HP and conditional sale

agreements, which allow the creditor to retain ownership of the goods supplied as security until all payments are made, extra protections are provided for debtors. In particular, once one-third of the total price of the goods has been paid, they become 'protected goods' and on default by the debtor can only be recovered through a repossession order granted by the county court. Creditors who ignore this will find they must repay all the money already received from the debtor and be unable to sue for any arrears. In addition, if the debtor terminates the agreement and returns the goods before all repayments are made, no more than 50% of the total price can be demanded by way of compensation, unless the goods have deteriorated more than is associated with fair wear and tear.

In any situation where the debtor defaults, a default notice must be sent giving the debtor seven days in which to put matters right, and if this is done no further action can be taken.

Apart from these provisions (which apply to all forms of credit including bank loans and overdrafts, HP and conditional sale agreements, credit sale agreements, money lending and pawnbroking,) the Act also regulates in detail the taking of securities and guarantees for loans and requires those involved to be given detailed information about the transaction.

11.8　Credit Facilities Available Only to Companies

Organisations which are in the business of supplying credit only for companies will not be affected by the requirements of the Consumer Credit Act, and are subject only to the general law of contract and the Companies Act, plus self-regulation imposed on such institutions by the City of London.

Companies often borrow money through issuing debentures, i.e. documents which are evidence of a loan or debt. Most debentures are secured, so that in the event of default the creditor has some asset of the company which is security for the loan. Registers of debenture holders are kept by the company and many have to be registered with the Registrar of Companies.

11.9　Insurance

Payments owed by businesses may be made not by them personally but by an insurance company on their behalf. Such insurance exists to pay money if a particular, unwelcome contingency occurs.

However, insurance companies will only pay out if their policy holder, i.e. the insured business, is under a legal obligation to pay. Many cases which reach the courts are in reality being fought out by insurance companies who wish to dispute their client's liability. Insurance companies will also only pay if the contingency is clearly covered by the policy, which has been correctly entered into.

The insurance agreement is primarily simply a contract between the insurance company and the insured person, whereby the insurer agrees to indemnify the other party against loss arising by the occurrence of the risk insured against, in return for payment of a fee known as the premium. The premium will rise if a large number of claims are made under the policy. However, it is a special kind of contract, one of the 'utmost good faith' *(uberrimae fidei)* which requires the insured to give the insurer all relevant information about the policy whether or not it is specifically requested by the insurance company. Any false information which may be given, either intentionally or not, has the effect of nullifying the agreement, as can any information which is not disclosed that the insurance company thinks is relevant. It is therefore vital that the proposal form issued by the insurer is fully and carefully answered, otherwise the insurance company may avoid liability. In *Dawsons Limited* v *Bonnin* [1922] 2 A.C. 413, the insured gave an incorrect answer to the question of where a lorry would be garaged. The wrong answer would have made no difference to the policy offered, but when the lorry was destroyed by fire in an accident which was not connected with the parking arrangements, the insurance company were held entitled to refuse to pay.

Some types of insurance are compulsory, for instance that taken up by employers to enable them to pay compensation to an employee injured at work, (see Chapter 13), and that for motor vehicles. Other insurance is left for the business to decide to have or not, for example to cover fire or other damage to business premises, or for product liability, see Sections 10.1–10.4.

Questions

1 What do you understand by the term legal tender?
2 What is the purpose and effect of 'crossing a cheque'?
3 Why might businesses sell their debts to a factor?
4 What types of agreements are covered by the Consumer Credit Act 1974?

5 Explain the meaning of the following terms and say what their importance is:
(a) APR (b) a cooling-off period for credit sales.

6 How does the licensing system under the Consumer Credit Act operate?
What other forms of licensing for businesses do you know of?
Do you think that licensing is an effective method of controlling business behaviour?

7 What is meant by a contract of the utmost good faith?

8 What types of insurance should a company have? Investigate the various types which are available and their cost.

9 Your business is considering offering credit facilities to its customers. Explain to them how the Consumer Credit Act may affect this operation and the obligations it would place on the business.

PART IV

THE LAW RELATING TO EMPLOYMENT

The basic relationship between employers and employees is contractual, and until the mid 1960s Parliament intervened very little in the regulation of this arrangement. Each side was free to make its own bargain. However, it became clear that, as with consumers and small businesses dealing with large organisations, it was a somewhat one-sided relationship as the employee had little power to negotiate on equal terms with the employer. Therefore the legislature introduced various Acts in order to strengthen the position of the employee.

This Part will look at the legal position of businesses when 'hiring and firing' employees, and also their responsibilities to one another during the course of the employment.

Chapter 12

Employing Staff

The following chapter will consider both Common Law and statutory obligations which relate to the recruiting of staff and the terms of their employment.

12.1 Advertising for Staff

When advertising for new employees it is important to be aware of the legislation which among other things prevents the overt discrimination against persons of a particular race or sex when appointing staff. The two pieces of legislation involved are the Race Relations Act 1976 and the Sex Discrimination Act 1975. Both Acts require that no intention to discriminate unlawfully is evidenced within the advertisement. Unlawful discrimination can be either direct or indirect – the difference is that direct discrimination is shown when someone is treated less favourably simply on the grounds of his or her race or sex, whereas indirect discrimination involves imposing an unjustifiable condition which more members of one sex or race can comply with than others. Examples of this might be advertisements stipulating that all applicants must be over five feet six inches tall, or to have blue eyes for no good reason connected with the job. When a job title is used which suggests that it is available to members of only one sex or race (e.g. Chinese waitress) this requirement must fall within the categories of a genuine occupational qualification, (GOQ) laid down in the Acts, or make it clear that men and women and people of all races can apply. There are only four GOQs for race as follows:

1. Authenticity of entertainment: e.g. Russian dancers.
2. Authenticity of modelling: e.g. for Singapore Airlines.
3. Authenticity of food and drink establishments: e.g. Chinese staff for a Chinese restaurant.

4. For work with a particular ethnic group: e.g. West Indian social worker to work within the West Indian community.

The GOQs to specify the sex of an individual are more numerous, but the most important of them are:

1. Authenticity of entertainment: e.g. actress to play Desdemona.
2. Decency or privacy: e.g. lavatory attendants or lighthouse keepers who have to live together.

The necessity for strength or stamina is not a GOQ as these are not exclusively found in one sex.

The requirements about advertising do not extend to small businesses employing five or fewer people or to private households in the case of sex discrimination.

As it is unlikely that individuals would be sufficiently moved to take action against such advertisements appearing, the task of keeping them under review and taking action if need be, is given to the two bodies set up by the legislation to oversee the working of the Acts, the Equal Opportunities Commission (EOC) and the Commission for Racial Equality (CRE) for sex and race discrimination respectively. Usually it is only necessary for the appropriate Commission to point out the breach of the law to the advertiser for this to be remedied, but if necessary a non-discrimination notice could be obtained through the courts for which a penalty could be imposed if breached in future. However, it is to be remembered in all considerations of the discrimination legislation that no criminal offences have been created by the two Acts.

12.2   Selecting Staff

(a) *Discrimination*

The provisions of the 1975 and 1976 Acts above also apply to the selection of staff. It is specifically unlawful to discriminate against someone directly or indirectly on the grounds of her or his sex or marital status (i.e. because the person is married, but perhaps surprisingly it is not unlawful to discriminate against someone because he or she is single or divorced) or on the grounds of their race in selection for a job, the terms on which this job is offered, and later in the training provided or promotion offered or dismissal (see further Section 14.3). For the purposes of the legislation, race is widely defined as including colour, race, ethnic or national origins, but does not directly include religion, although this may be covered if the person's religion defines them as part of a recognisable racial group such as Sikhs and Jews.

It is, however, very difficult for an unsuccessful job candidate to prove that discrimination has taken place. Although the appropriate Commission would be available to advise on a case of this sort it is unlikely to take up the case on the complainant's behalf unless it is seen as an important test case or there is evidence of widespread discrimination in that organisation, when a general investigation would be carried out. At the end of this a non-discrimination notice might be issued, ordering the business to desist from its discriminatory action for the five-year duration of the notice. However this would not benefit the individual directly and it would be necessary to take a case to the industrial tribunal to gain compensation if discrimination could be shown. (For procedures of tribunals see Sections 2.7 and 14.4).

The employer is under no obligation to release confidential documents to the complainant, but a series of written questions can be submitted to the employer. It is advisable to answer these fully, as any failure to do so can be taken into account at the subsequent tribunal hearing. Also at this stage it may become obvious to the complainant that no discrimination was involved in his or her failure to obtain the job. From the employee's point of view, it may be easier to take a case based on discrimination during the course of employment, as there may be more access to and awareness of proof of discrimination, but this is countered by the inherent difficulties in taking one's employer through legal proceedings!

Should the case proceed to a hearing, and the complainant prove that discrimination has occurred, the tribunal has the power to order one of three remedies. These are:

1. The issue of a statement setting out that discrimination has occurred and declaring the rights of the claimant.

2. Ordering the employer to pay compensation.

3. A recommendation that the employer remedies the situation, which if not done can lead to further compensation being payable.

The amount of compensation awarded in such cases is usually very low although it may include elements for hurt feelings in circumstances when little actual monetary loss can be shown.

Few successful cases have been taken under this legislation, but its effects may be seen in that expressions of overt discrimination in job advertisements or interviews have more or less ceased and this has led to a reduction in stereotyping. Indeed, some organisations have taken positive initiatives to encourage under-represented groups such as women and ethnic minorities to apply for jobs and promotions. It must be emphasised, however, that there is no legal duty to do so, and no positive discrimination legislation has been introduced requiring quotas of such groups to be employed, as has been done in other countries such as the United States. Indeed the introduction of schemes of that sort may well amount to unlawful discrimination against the other sex or races, although special training schemes and initiatives for under-represented members of one sex or race are permissible.

It is also worth noting that discrimination on grounds other than sex, marital status and occasionally trade union membership (see Section 14.3), for instance requiring certain standards of dress, or qualifications or even an age limit, is only unlawful if it can be shown to be a method, albeit unconscious, of indirect sex or race discrimination. Advertisement for 'attractive young bar staff' and such like are therefore perfectly legitimate as beauty, of course, is in the eye of the beholder!

The only exception to the rule about quotas is that every business employing more than twenty people is required to employ a minimum of 3% of registered disabled people among its workforce.

(b) Taking up references

Most employers will require references when making a decision on who to appoint, but how much reliance can be placed on those obtained? No specific laws govern this area and there is certainly no requirement that an ex-employer or other person should give a reference. However, once it is given, it should be a truthful assessment of the candidate's capabilities as it involves publication to a third party, i.e. the prospective employer, and is therefore subject to an action for *libel* by the maligned individual if it should include false and dishonourable information. The libelled person would have no right to see the document and may therefore never discover its contents. A misled employer would have no action against the writer in contract (as there was no consideration for the requirement to give the reference and therefore no contract existed) and would have difficulty in establishing an action for negligence or other tort such as deceit, especially as any direct recoverable loss may be difficult to establish, although in theory it may be possible to take such an action.

The giving of false information during an interview or on an application form could of course amount to a criminal offence if the intention was to deceive and may well, subject to *(c)* below, be grounds for subsequent dismissal (see Section 14.3). A deceptively favourable reference may also be an imprisonable offence by virtue of the Theft Act.

(c) Rehabilitation of offenders

In the past it has been difficult for those who have received criminal convictions and have paid their 'debt to society' by fulfilling a prison term or other sentence, to find employment afterwards as a result of their record. To try to overcome this, the Rehabilitation of Offenders Act 1974 allows for convictions to become 'spent' after a certain amount of time. This means that they do not have to be disclosed at interviews or on application forms; they have in effect been wiped off the record. Examples of the time required for convictions to be 'spent' are as follows:

A term of imprisonment up to six months–spent after seven years. Conditional discharge or probation–spent after one year.

Some types of serious convictions are never spent and some jobs because of their nature are exempt from the Act and thus any convictions must always be disclosed. Such jobs include teaching, social work, the police, etc.

12.3 The Employment Contract

A contract of employment exists from the moment two parties reach agreement on the basic terms. There is, as with most contracts, no requirement for this to be evidenced formally in writing, although in practice this is usually done. At the time of writing a formal offer letter many employers take the opportunity of complying with the requirements of the Employment Protection (Consolidation) Act 1978 relating to a written statement of the terms of employment. This legislation requires that certain, but not necessarily all, of the terms of a person's contract be supplied to her or him in writing during the first thirteen weeks of employment. This is in order that both parties have a record of the fundamental terms to refer to in the event of dispute over the exact nature of the job for which the employee was taken on, or length of service for calculating redundancy pay, etc. The matters which must be dealt with are as follows:

(a) Names of the employer and employee.
(b) The date when the employment began.
(c) Whether any previous employment counts towards the employee's period of continuous employment.
(d) Date at which contract expires if it is for a fixed term.
(e) Rate of pay.
(f) Interval, e.g. weekly, monthly, when pay is made.
(g) Hours of work.
(h) Holidays and holiday pay, sick pay and pension rights.
(i) Length of notice which the employee must give and is entitled to receive.
(j) A statement about the disciplinary and grievance procedure operating in the business, or information about where details of these may be found.

Additional terms may and probably will have been agreed during the interview, for example the availability of a training course, and are all part of the contract, but there is no requirement that this be in writing. However a wise employee should ask for these to be recorded as proof that such commitments were made. There is no obligation on employees to sign the written statement, except to acknowledge that it has been received and indeed this should not be required as it may then appear that no further terms of the contract exist. Changes in the terms of employment should be notified in writing within one month.

Any employer who fails to provide the written statement within the required period can be taken to an industrial tribunal by the affected employee for an order to be granted setting out this duty, although no compensation may be awarded.

Apart from the express terms agreed between the parties, the mere existence of the contract gives rise to implied terms. On the part of the employer, these would include the obligation to provide work agreed upon, to pay the employee and generally to act in a reasonable manner towards the employee. The employee would be obliged to work to his or her ability with reasonable care and skill, and to serve the employer faithfully. This would involve not disclosing trade secrets or poaching the employer's customers and clients both during and even after employment. In order to strengthen this requirement, many employers include an express term in some contracts, restraining their ex-employees from working for a rival company, or in a certain area, within a period of time after leaving their employment. This may be used in contracts in such trades as hairdressing where clients' loyalty is built up, or for high-ranking members of the business who are privy to much commercial information of use to rivals. Such a restriction, although viewed severely by the courts, will be upheld if it is deemed to be 'reasonable' both between the parties and in relation to the public interest as a whole. For example in the case of *Home Counties Dairies Limited* v *Skilton* [1970] 1 All E.R. 1227 a restraint on a milkman, who agreed that for a year after leaving his job he would not sell milk to customers of his previous company, was held to be reasonable as it was necessary to protect his company from losing customers.

The remedy a company could apply for to enforce the restriction would be an injunction ordering the ex-employee not to break the terms of the contract. This would be of far more use to the company than an award of damages after the harm had already been inflicted. Great care should be exercised when inserting such clauses to ensure that they do not go further than absolutely necessary to protect a legitimate interest and do not unreasonably restrict the individual's right to earn a living and pursue his or her career. Otherwise the courts will rule that the clause is invalid as an unreasonable restraint of trade, and no smaller restriction would be imposed. The result would be that the employee would be free to work immediately for whomsoever and wherever he or she chose.

12.4 Employee or Independent Contractor?

There are a number of reasons why it might be important to decide whether the person employed should be regarded as an employee or as an independent contractor, i.e. someone not directly under the control and responsibility of the employer, although working for the employer for a period of time. Perhaps the most obvious reason is that in the latter case the employer will not be responsible for such matters as payment of national insurance and tax, nor will the contract between them amount to a contract of employment. Therefore such obligations as the written statement and the law relating to dismissal and redundancy (see Chapter 14) will not apply. Additionally it is a Common Law rule that all employers are vicariously liable for torts committed by employees in the course of their employment, but not for the actions of independent contractors. See further Section 13.2.

It may therefore be significant in a number of cases to determine what form the relationship takes, and in this the law has its own rules, and does not entirely depend on whether the parties designate the worker as self-employed, independent contractor or whatever. The test used by the courts will rely on three factors:

   (i) control
 (ii) integration into the organisation
(iii) the economic reality of the situation.

The first is the oldest test and was applied by determining how much control the employer had over the way the worker carried out the job. Where the workers had freedom to decide how (but not whether) to perform the allotted task, the worker would be regarded as an independent contractor. As organisations became larger, this test on its own became more unrealistic, and the other two factors were added. The integration test, as the name implies, examines how far the worker is an integral part of the organisation, or how far outside the main functions of the organisation he or she remains. The final test takes the broadest view of all and looks at all relevant factors, including how the employer and worker have dealt with such matters as appointment, payment, hours of work and provision of tools and equipment. Each case will therefore be regarded on its merits. A simple example to explain the difference in practice is to compare the role of the taxi driver with the chauffeur; the latter is an employee whereas the former is an independent contractor, although both will perform the same function of transporting their employer from A to B.

12.5   Pay

As mentioned previously, the employer is under an implied duty to pay the employee. The amount due is normally subject only to agreement between them as laid down in the contract i.e. it depends on what the parties themselves had agreed at the initial interview or later during job evaluation. Sometimes the rates of pay will be settled by collective bargaining between the workers' representatives on one side and management on the other. This may be done on a plant-by-plant basis, or nationally when the employers' associations negotiate with the large trade unions to set rates of pay throughout a particular industry. The shared feature of this process is that it is unfettered by the law and depends solely on the negotiating strength of the parties involved.

The absence of the law from this area is subject to two important exceptions as outlined in *(a)* and *(b)* below.

(a) Wages Councils

Contrary to popular belief, there is no statutory minimum pay level below which wages cannot fall, although government figures on poverty levels are often issued as a guideline. However, in industries covered by Wages Councils, minimum rates of pay are laid down and it is a criminal offence to pay workers at lower rates. Wages Councils currently serve approximately twenty-five industries although their powers have been cut down quite considerably in recent years. They are found in industries, such as retailing and garment making, where traditionally very low rates of pay were paid and where the workers were weak, scattered and therefore subject to exploitation. This legislation, now governed by the Wages Act 1986, is policed by a specialised Wages Inspectorate. The regulations made under the Act are detailed, although they have now been simplified and no longer apply to young people under the age of twenty-one.

(b) Equal pay

Traditionally women have earned lower rates of pay than men and in the wake of the women's liberation movement came pressure for this situation to be remedied. The Equal Pay Act was passed in 1970, although it did not come into force until 1975, and went some way towards achieving this. The legislation states that an implied term known as the 'equality clause' is deemed to be included in the contract of every woman employee, entitling her to similar rates of pay, holiday and other benefits to those for male employees in the same organisation where she can prove one of the following applies:

  (i) She and the male are employed to do like or broadly similar work.
 (ii) She and the male are doing work rated as equivalent by a job evaluation scheme.
(iii) She and the male are doing work of equal value to the organisation. Whether this is so will ultimately be determined by an independent expert appointed by an industrial tribunal.

The first requirement is restricted to where men and women are doing practically the same job. The second requirement has as a prerequisite, the carrying out of a job evaluation scheme, but there is no obligation to instigate such a scheme. The original legislation contained only these two provisions and very few successful cases were brought. Even when a woman could show she had *more* responsibility than a man she still had no right to equal pay. The third provision was introduced in 1984 as a result of rulings in the European Court of Justice that our legislation did not meet with the requirement of the EEC Treaty and directives made under it relating to equal treatment of men and women.

It is therefore now possible for women doing work of a totally different nature to their male colleagues to claim that they have a right to be paid at the same level. The assessment of this will be based on factors such as level of qualifications required, responsibility, skill, etc. In the first case to be heard relating to this provision, *Hayward* v *Cammell Laird Limited* [1984] I.R.L.R. 463, Ms Hayward, a cook, was held to be entitled to the same pay and entitlement as various male craftsmen employed by the shipyard.

The introduction of this legislation, particularly the amendment in 1984 relating to work of equal value, has given women a strong negotiating tool which they can use to try to improve their pay levels. However, if nothing can be achieved through negotiation, the individual woman concerned must take her case to the industrial tribunal either during employment or within six months of leaving, for them to decide on its merits. Should the decision go in her favour, the tribunal can declare that the supposed equality clause exists, and award back pay for a maximum period of two years.

It should be noted, however, that this legislation does not allow the tribunal to set general levels of pay. It is limited to comparisons between men and women within the same employment, and if the workforce is all one sex no claim can be made. In addition, no claim can be based on rates of pay which apply elsewhere, even within the same industry, whether these are earned by men or women.

(c) Methods of pay

All employees are entitled to an itemised pay statement setting out in writing how their pay has been calculated. During sickness, entitlement to pay will depend on the terms of the employee's contract, but most employees will be entitled to Statutory Sick Pay from the State scheme out of their national insurance contributions, but which is administered by the employer for the first eight weeks of illness.

In the interest of efficiency and to prevent wages' robberies, recent legislation has abolished the right of workers to demand to be paid in cash.

(d) Guaranteed pay

If no work is available for an employee and the employer has written into the contract the right to withhold pay in these circumstances, an employee is still entitled to a maximum of five days pay in any three-month period with a variable daily maximum. This would not apply during a strike, or if the employee refused alternative work or had not been employed for at least a month. Trade unions may negotiate better rates.

12.6 Maternity Rights

Any woman employee who becomes pregnant is entitled to reasonable time off with pay to attend ante-natal care appointments. In addition any woman who has completed at least two years' continuous employment with the same employer eleven weeks before the birth will be entitled to some maternity pay and leave, with the right to return to her old job within twenty-nine weeks of the birth. This right is subject to the correct notice of her intentions. Dismissal solely due to pregnancy will normally be automatically unfair (see further Section 14.3).

12.7 Trade Union Membership

It is *not* unlawful for an employer to refuse to employ someone on the ground of their trade union membership or non-membership. However, once in employment everyone has a right to join the trade union of his or her own choice, although the employer may or may not 'recognise' the union for bargaining purposes. It is unlawful for an employer to penalise an employee for joining or taking part in the activities of an independent trade union, i.e. one not controlled by the employer, at an appropriate time. Ordinary employees are entitled to reasonable time off *without* pay to take part in the activities of a recognised trade union, for example attending meetings. Officials such as shop stewards are entitled to reasonable time off *with* pay to attend to their duties and go on training courses. What is reasonable will depend on what has been negotiated between the parties, or implied by custom and practice in that workplace, and ACAS has produced a code of practice which gives guidance, though no more than this, on these rights.

Except where a 'closed shop' exists an employee also has the right not to belong to a union and to have no action taken against him or her because of it. Where a closed shop, or officially a 'union membership agreement', exists, whereby the employer has agreed to employ only members of a specified union or unions, an employee can be dismissed for refusing to join, unless he or she was in the employment before the agreement came into effect or has deeply held personal convictions, perhaps religious or otherwise, against joining. A closed shop can only be enforced if it has the support of 80% of those entitled to vote in a secret ballot or 85% of those actually voting, and this support must be renewed at least every five years.

Dismissal relating to trade union membership will be dealt with in Section 14.3.

12.8   Industrial Action

When employees go on strike they are usually breaking their contracts of employment. However, it is rarely appropriate for employers to sue individual employees, but they may take action against individuals or trade unions who organise the strike and thereby cause loss. However, such bodies have immunity from liability if the action is lawful and has been carried out 'in contemplation or furtherance of a trade dispute'. This would mean that it was primarily concerned with matters to do with conditions of employment, such as wages or hours of work, and action is being taken directly against the employer and not, for instance, against customers or suppliers (so called 'sympathy strikes'). The strike would also have to be preceded by a valid secret ballot of the workforce. The court can issue injunctions to prevent unlawful actions, and if these are not complied with, large fines can be imposed on unions and officials for contempt of court. However, many businesses consider that legal action against their own workforce will only lead to worse industrial relations in the future and do not make use of their legal rights.

Strikers who are dismissed during a strike cannot normally complain of unfair dismissal, see Section 14.3.

Strikes rarely involve criminal offences, although associated actions like picketing may result in prosecution for violent or abusive behaviour or obstructing the police or the highway.

The government agency ACAS can be used to provide a neutral arbitration service to settle industrial relations disputes amicably between employers and employees.

Questions

1 What terms must be included in the written statement of the terms of employment, and what is the function of this document?

2 Explain the effects of the following:
   (a) restraint of trade clauses,
   (b) equality clauses.

3 To discriminate against someone on the grounds of her or his sex or race is a criminal offence. True or false?

4 Distinguish between an employee and an independent contractor. When would this distinction be important?

5 To what extent does the law give everyone the right to belong to a trade union?

6 During the 1960s, legislation was introduced which has since been repealed which attempted to regulate both rates of pay and prices – a so-called prices and incomes policy. What would be the benefits and drawbacks of such legislation and do you think it would be justified?

7 Is the following advertisement lawful? If not, why not and how could it be rephrased in order to comply with the legislation?
   SWEDISH WAITRESSES REQUIRED FOR DIRECTORS' DINING ROOM

8 Joe applies to go on a training course within a company which could lead to promotion. He and two others apply for the two places on the course, but he is not selected. He feels that, as he has been employed for a year longer than his colleagues, he should have had priority, but that he has not been selected because he is a refugee from Vietnam and the others are British. Advise him as to his legal rights in this situation and what his best course of action would be.

9 Jane and Jenny are typists who have recently been trained to use word processors. They feel that they should receive the same salary as the computer operators, who at present earn £50 a month more than them. Advise them.

Chapter 13

Safety at Work

Historically the role of the law in ensuring that workplaces were reasonably safe for employees was confined to the civil law process of compensating for injury after it occurred with the mildly deterrent effect that the possibility of such action had on employers. However, it was soon recognised that this was not enough to prevent accidents occurring in the increasingly mechanised workplaces of the nineteenth century, and additional criminal penalties were introduced to enforce standards of safety in some industries. These two systems still work side-by-side to try to guarantee a reasonably safe work environment, and this chapter will examine both in turn and assess their effectiveness.

13.1 Actions against the Employer in Negligence

It has long been established that employers owe a duty of care to their employees while they are at work which, if breached, could give rise to an action in tort for negligence. There is also an implied contractual duty to provide a reasonably safe working environment. The standard required is simply that of a 'reasonable' employer in the position of that particular employer, bearing in mind all the circumstances of the case. This, therefore, varies from situation to situation, and would for example require an employer to take special precautions when an employee was particularly vulnerable. So where employers knew that a worker had only one good eye they were held negligent when special goggles were not provided to prevent injury to the other eye: *Paris* v *Stepney Borough Council* [1951] A.C. 367. The normal duty would involve ensuring that the workforce was reasonably carefully selected, trained and supervised, that plant was of a reasonable quality and reasonably maintained, and that systems of work were reasonably safe to implement.

142

An action in negligence involves the plaintiff in proving not only that the duty was owed, and that it was breached, but also that injury was caused to him or her as a direct result. This means that a case can only be brought after the event has occurred and does not act as a major encouragement of safe working practices. It also means that individual employees have to take action against their own employers, not always a course an individual would wish to undertake, apart from the difficulties in proving that 'reasonable care' had not been taken.

A partial defence is available to employers in a negligence action in that if negligence is proved, but the injured employee had played a part in the accident, then the amount of damages awarded may be reduced in proportion to the employee's contributory negligence. Thus an award of £100 000 may be reduced to £70 000 if the employee was held to be 30% to blame.

Most employers prudently insured against such liability (thereby of course decreasing the incentive to ensure safe working conditions to a certain extent), and since the Employers' Liability (Compulsory Insurance) Act 1969 this has been a legal requirement. The majority of actions are settled without the need to resort to court, perhaps as a result of trade union intervention on behalf of an injured employee. However, the impression should not be given that all accidents at work will give rise to successful compensation claims, as the standard of reasonable care requires there to have been an element of fault on the part of someone other than the employee before liability will be admitted.

13.2   Vicarious Liability

In addition to employers being directly liable to employees for their lapses from standards of reasonable care for safety, they may also be held to be vicariously liable for the negligence of *other* employees. This concept means that they are held responsible for the actions of others, although they themselves may be in no way at fault. This places an additional responsibility on employers to ensure care in the selection and supervision of staff.

Vicarious liability arises only when torts are committed in the course of employment. These include activities which have specifically been prohibited by the management but which still take place within the terms of the employment. So employers have been held responsible for the negligent driving of two bus drivers who had been forbidden to race their vehicles towards a particularly narrow stretch of road, but who continued to do so and caused an accident. On the other hand, employees who are off 'on a frolic of their own', albeit during working hours, such as a van driver taking a detour to drop off a personal package on the way back from an authorised journey, do not render their employers vicariously liable for their activities.

Anyone injured as a result of negligence by an employee, be they a fellow-employee, a pedestrian or whatever, therefore has a choice of actions – against the individual for negligence or against the vicariously liable employer. In each case it would be necessary to show that the employee had fallen below the standards of care required, i.e. that of a reasonable person in those particular circumstances, and in addition, if the latter course of action was pursued, that this occurred during the course of employment. For obvious practical reasons it is often better to sue a business rather than an individual person. In theory, the employer could recover any compensation payable from the employee, but in practice this is rarely done, particularly if in the meantime, as is likely, the employee has been dismissed.

13.3   Employer's Liability (Defective Equipment) Act 1969

Employees often experienced difficulties (in common with other plaintiffs in negligence actions, see also Section 10.3) in identifying those who might have shown an absence of reasonable care when injured by defective equipment at work. The employers might have been able to show that they themselves had taken reasonable care in that they had bought from reputable suppliers and perhaps tested the equipment adequately in advance, leaving the injured worker to find the culprit. As a result, the 1969 Act was passed which makes employers strictly liable for injuries caused by defective equipment supplied for use at work. This means that the employee only has to prove the equipment to be defective, and the employer will be responsible to pay compensation. It is then open to the employer to pursue a remedy against the supplier of the equipment if this is feasible.

13.4   The Factories Act and Related Legislation

In the nineteenth century campaigners began to try to rid British industry of the many dangerous working practices that had developed during the industrial revolution. Gradually, and in a piecemeal fashion, legislation was introduced to require certain standards to be maintained in specified industries, these standards to be enforced by government inspectors backed up by criminal penalties. By 1972 there were eleven major statutes and nearly five hundred statutory instruments covering industries ranging from factories, mines and quarries, agriculture and offices, shops and railway premises.

These Acts, which remain as part of the law today, varied according to the needs of the particular industry, but the feature they had in common was that on the whole they were tightly and rigidly defined to relate only to those areas. Thus for instance, in order for a workplace to be governed by the Factories Act 1961, it must be:

> 'premises in which persons are employed in manual labour in specified processes associated with making, altering or adapting an article for sale, or in slaughtering animals, and where the work is carried out by way of trade or for purposes of gain and over which the employer has a right of access or control'.

Some activities therefore fall outside this definition, such as workshops in an educational establishment.

The legislation then goes on to provide a very detailed set of requirements which must be met in such premises. These include general matters like ventilation, lighting, cleanliness and space available to each employee, first-aid and welfare provisions, and specific safety measures such as the fencing of machinery and the construction and maintenance of certain equipment. These are often backed up by even more detailed regulations. Breach of any of these requirements is a criminal offence for which large fines and even imprisonment may be imposed. In addition, many of the provisions allow for anyone injured to sue for breach of statutory duty. The injury would have to be caused by a direct breach of the legislation so, for instance, a worker was unable to claim when he was injured by a piece of machinery flying off and hitting him, although he would have been able to claim if he had injured himself on non-guarded machinery.

These statutory provisions provide a fair measure of protection. However, they were subject to two important limitations. Firstly they only applied to clearly defined workplaces and therefore approximately eight million people at work were not protected. Secondly they adopt the 'check-list' approach to safety which means that no more is required than that which is specifically laid down in the legislation and regulations. After this has been complied with, no further efforts to provide a safe working environment is required by the criminal law.

For these reasons and the need to provide a comprehensive, integrated approach to safety at work, new legislation was introduced in 1974.

13.5   The Health and Safety at Work, etc. Act 1974

This Act may eventually replace all the previous legislation, but at present it exists alongside it. This means that those people who work in factories, offices, etc. are protected by at least two separate pieces of legislation. The 1974 Act applies to nearly all workplaces and imposes more general responsiblities on employers and others in regard to safety. It represents a move away from the 'check-list' approach to the 'systems' approach, putting the emphasis on each individual workplace to decide its own standards and levels of safety to match its own needs.

The main responsibility placed on employers by the Act is found in section 2 which states:

> 'It shall be the duty of every employer to ensure, so far as is reasonably practicable, the health, safety and welfare of all his employees.'

This includes among other things provision and maintenance of plant and systems of work that are safe and without risk to health, the provision of information, instructions, training and supervision, maintenance of safe places of work with risk-free means of access and egress, adequate welfare facilities and arrangements. Reasonable practicability will involve taking into account the costs of the safety measures involved, but because it varies from situation to situation an employer can never be sure that enough has been done. This is perhaps the main strength and weakness of the legislation, as it requires constant vigilance to comply with the Act.

A specific duty placed on employers is to draw up a written safety policy which must be given to every employee in businesses where five or more people are employed. This would lay down the general approach to safety plus the way this is to be implemented and must be kept up-to-date. This in itself would not be enough, however, as the Act places emphasis on the training and supervision of staff, and clearly it would be extremely good evidence of a breach of the Act if the business's own policy was not followed.

In addition the Act puts responsibility on occupiers of workplaces to ensure that those who live near or visit the workplace are reasonably safe, and that outside contractors are given adequate instructions and warnings when engaged on work within the plant. Those who manufacture or design equipment for use at work are also required to ensure that it is as safe as is reasonably practicable (see also Section 10.8).

The Act is supplemented by very detailed regulations and also codes of practice drawn up by the Health and Safety Commission (see below) which give guidance on good practice. Breach of any of these requirements (apart from those in the codes of practice) is a criminal offence, and there is no need for an accident to have occurred for an offence to be committed. In effect, the legislation has transferred the existing civil law duty of employers in negligence, as set out in Section 13.1 above, to the criminal law. This sometimes causes confusion, as the tests for liability are very similar, but the Health and Safety at Work Act makes it clear that no civil actions for breach of statutory duty can be taken based solely on the Act. However, in a civil action for negligence, evidence of lack of adherence to the safety policy or, even better, a relevant conviction would obviously be useful to show a want of reasonable care. (It should be noted that the corresponding *civil* duty of occupiers of premises to visitors and neighbours is laid down in the Occupiers' Liability Acts 1957 to 1984).

13.6 Employees' Responsibilities

The responsibilities under the Acts so far considered have been of the employers, manufacturers of work equipment or occupiers of business premises. However, the 1974 Act also emphasises the responsibility and involvement of the workforce, from the managing director down to the most junior employee. Specifically the Act requires that employees take reasonable care for the health and safety of themselves and others, they co-operate with their employer over safety matters, and they do not misuse or interfere with things provided for health and safety. Breach of these duties would be a criminal offence, punishable by a fine or possibly even imprisonment. It is unlikely that an individual employee would be prosecuted however unless there was clear evidence of reckless disregard of others' safety and/or failure to follow clear and specific instructions.

The Act also encourages the involvement of the workforce to ensure their own working environment is as safe as possible through the provision for the establishment of safety representatives and safety committees. Recognised trade unions are given the right to .appoint safety representatives, who should usually have at least two years' experience in that workplace, whose responsibility it is to negotiate with the management on safety matters. In order to do this their duties involve investigating and inspecting potential hazards and complaints from fellow-workers. They are entitled to reasonable time off with pay to perform these functions. In addition, two or more safety representatives can request in writing for a safety committee to be set up containing representatives from both the workforce and management as a forum to discuss and administer safety matters.

It should be noted that the right to have safety representatives is limited to workplaces where a recognised trade union exists. However, there is nothing to prevent non-unionised workplaces from appointing equivalent representatives, after negotiation with management, to fulfil the duties under the Act. In addition it is quite usual for businesses to appoint a management representative, perhaps called the Safety Officer, who, though not required by law, will have responsibility for safety matters in general.

13.7 Health and Safety Commission and Executive

The Health and Safety Commission is a government agency with overall responsibility for safety at work. In addition to drawing up codes of practice for guidance, it initiates research and ensures that the government has adequate information about the necessity for new regulations. It also has overall responsibility for the Health and Safety Executive.

The Executive is the enforcement body of the Act and is responsible for the teams of inspectors who have the day-to-day responsibility for ensuring that businesses abide by the Health and Safety at Work Act. The old specialised inspectorates, such as factories inspectors and mines and quarries inspectors, are now all under the one organisation but retain their specialist functions on the whole.

Inspectors have the power to enter premises at any reasonable time or when there is danger, can examine books and documents and investigate any relevant matters. Recently the role of the inspectorate as an advisory and consultative body has been stressed, but this sits uncomfortably with their responsibilities to enforce the Act through prosecution or the issuing of prohibition or improvement notices.

Inspectors have the power to prosecute for any breach of the Act which they discover, whether or not an accident has occurred. Punishment would be in the form of a fine or in exceptional cases imprisonment of an individual. However, this course of action is rarely adopted, and the fines imposed are generally low enough not to act as a very effective deterrent. The imposition of improvement or prohibition notices is viewed by inspectors and businesses alike as a far more effective method of enforcement. As its name implies, an improvement notice can be issued requiring that a piece of machinery, building or process of work be improved within a certain period of time. Where there is a risk of serious personal injury, a prohibition notice can be issued requiring that the stated activity should not be carried on until remedied. Breach of such notices is a criminal offence in itself, and although appeal is possible through an industrial tribunal, very few are successful. Complying with the notices can be very costly for the business concerned, particularly if a manufacturing process has to be interrupted in order to do so.

When the Act was first introduced, businesses were very worried about the cost of meeting their obligations under the Act, particularly as there was no way of knowing when enough had been done to satisfy the requirement of reasonable practicability. In recent years, however, with cutbacks among the inspectorate and the loss of bargaining power by some trade union safety representatives lessening the impact of the internal pressure for higher safety standards, these fears have receded somewhat. It is possible that in the future smaller businesses may be exempted from the full force of the Health and Safety at Work Act as part of the process of 'lifting the burden' on businesses.

Questions

1 What civil law responsibility does an employer owe to an employee with regard to the latter's safety at work?
2 Explain how the concept of vicarious liability operates in the area of safety at work.
3 How does the Health and Safety at Work Act seek to improve on

the previous legislative and judicial attempts to ensure a safe working environment? How successful has it been?

4 What is the importance of the written safety policy?

5 Explain the role played by the following in health and safety at work:
safety representatives
safety committees
health and safety inspectors.

6 Go back to Question 7 in Chapter 2 and write a fuller account of the legal position in this situation.

7 If you have a job, find and read your own written safety policy. What steps are taken at your workplace to ensure that it is implemented? Do you know who your safety representatives are (if any)? Find out what they have been involved in lately.

Chapter 14

Dismissal and Redundancy

This chapter will examine the legal obligations placed on employers when a contract of employment comes to an end. Until relatively recently this was left very much to the two parties to arrange for themselves, but a recognition of the inequality of bargaining positions led the legislature to intervene on behalf of the weaker party, the employee. The extent of this protection is sometimes exaggerated, however, and the following explanation will attempt to give a balanced view of the position of both parties.

14.1 Notice

Notice is usually required by either party to bring the employment contract to an end. The length of this may be included in the contract but, if none is specified, then statutory minima have been laid down in the Employment Protection (Consolidation) Act 1978. These are as follows:

Notice from employer to employee: after working from four weeks to two years – one week's notice. Each year after, one additional week to a maximum of twelve after twelve years' service.

Notice from employee to employer: minimum one week regardless of length of service.

The notice does not have to be in any particular form and could be given orally. Payment in lieu of notice may be an acceptable alternative to both parties.

Dismissal of an employee without the correct notice on grounds other than gross misconduct might lead to a claim being brought by the ex-employee for wrongful dismissal (see below), and would be taken into account by a tribunal when judging if this dismissal was carried out reasonably (see Section 14.3). In theory an employee who leaves without notice could be sued for breach of contract but in practice this rarely, if ever, happens.

14.2   Wrongful Dismissal

Before the introduction of the statutory concept of unfair dismissal in 1971 the only claim an employee had when 'fired' was for wrongful dismissal and this could only be maintained when incorrect notice was given. No concept of the job as a property right existed and a dismissal preceded by the correct notice (or instantly if gross misconduct was involved) could never be challenged. The Common Law right to take an action for wrongful dismissal still exists today, but would rarely be brought, the unfair dismissal claim being available to many more employees. As the remedy for a successful Common Law action is limited to the payment of salary or wages for the amount of notice lost, it is only really worthwhile for those entitled to three months' or so notice, or where a fixed-term contract is abruptly terminated. However, it may be important for an employee who has not worked the necessary qualifying period to claim unfair dismissal to clear his or her name of the imputation of gross misconduct by suing for wrongful dismissal.

Actions for wrongful dismissal are heard in the county court. The usual defence would be for the employer to state that no notice was required as the employee had acted in such a way as to strike at the root of the contractual relationship so that it could no longer continue. This would often be referred to as gross misconduct, and might involve theft of property, swearing, insubordination or other unacceptable behaviour. However, no hard-and-fast rules can be laid down as to what might amount to gross misconduct warranting summary dismissal 'on the spot' as this will vary in different situations. For example, swearing at or in front of customers or clients may be sufficient grounds, whereas using the same language among colleagues of a similar age and sex may not.

It should be noted that instant dismissal may also give rise to a claim for unfair dismissal. Lack of notice would simply be one of the factors taken into account when considering how the dismissal was carried out.

Employers who wish to discourage particular behaviour, e.g. smoking where this might be dangerous, would be advised to include a term in contracts stating that such action could result in instant dismissal. Provided that the policy was then carried out consistently, and the breach sufficiently important, a sacked employee would have few grounds for complaint.

14.3   Unfair Dismissal

Anyone employed since June 1985 has to work two years continuously for over sixteen hours a week for the same employer before any claim for unfair dismissal can be made. Those who work less than sixteen hours but more than eight for a continuous period of five years are entitled to make a claim, but those who work less than eight are never entitled to do so. In effect this means that employers have a period of two years in which to discover if an employee is suitable or not. Before this time there can be no comeback for any dismissal with proper notice unless a case of sexual or racial discrimination can be made out, or the grounds of dismissal are trade union membership or activities (see below). The law is found in the Employment Protection (Consolidation) Act 1978 as amended.

A claim for unfair dismissal must be taken to an industrial tribunal and be lodged within three months of the dismissal. A dismissal must have occurred either in the normal way by the employer terminating the contract or not renewing a fixed-term contract or, more unusually, through a 'constructive' dismissal. This is where the employee leaves because he or she has been put in a situation where there is no alternative, perhaps by being put under intolerable pressure by the employer or asked to undertake tasks for which he or she was not employed. At a tribunal hearing, the employer would be obliged to show that the dismissal was for a fair reason. These are laid down in the 1978 Act and are as follows:

1. Conduct.
2. Capability – including health.
3. Redundancy.
4. Legal prohibition e.g. lorry driver who loses licence.
5. Any other substantial reason.

Having established the reason for the dismissal was a fair one, the tribunal would then have to satisfy itself that the employer acted 'reasonably' in treating that reason as sufficient for dismissing the employee, 'having regard to equity and the substantial merits of the case'. The manner of the dismissal would be examined. For this purpose, the tribunal would look at various factors including whether the company's own disciplinary procedure and the ACAS codes of practice have been followed. Normally when discipline or incapability are involved, the tribunal would want to see evidence of the fact that the standards being achieved by the employee were unsatisfactory had been brought to the worker's attention, and giving him or her a chance to improve or explain. This might involve providing training facilities for under-achieving employees. Informal discussions on these points may be followed by a more formal written warning of failings, always with a chance for the employee to respond to any allegations. However, it must be emphasised that there are no hard-and-fast rules on this, each case will vary and the tribunal will take all relevant circumstances into account when reaching its decision. Factors the legislation is required to take into account are the size and administrative resources of the employer's business.

Because each case is judged very much on its own merits, previous decisions of industrial tribunals do not create precedents in the same way that ordinary court decisions do, although they will be useful to consider as guidelines. The following case illustrates how similar facts can lead to a different outcome because of individual circumstances—*Hallett and Want* v *MAT Transport* [1976]. Both Mr Hallett and Mr Want had been late for work and had received two written warnings for this. Subsequently Mr Want was late on twelve occasions out of eighty days while Mr Hallett was late on seven occasions out of seventy-seven days, three of these occasions due to industrial action on the railways. He had been employed for one and a half years and his record was improving. Both men were dismissed. Mr Want's dismissal was held to be fair while Mr Hallet's was unfair.

Illness will not in itself merit dismissal but, depending on the nature of the work and the employer's business, there will come a time when the employer is justified in giving the employee reasonable time to get fit and return to normal duties or other appropriate work, or else be fairly dismissed.

Appeals from industrial tribunals are heard by the Employment Appeals Tribunal, which has the status of the High Court and deals with questions of law. These decisions therefore may form precedents. In two circumstances, dismissal is automatically deemed to be unfair—when due to membership of, or involvement in, the activities of a trade union, or to refusal to join a valid 'closed shop' union without cause (see Section 12.7 for what constitutes a valid closed shop). No qualifying period of employment is necessary, and extra compensation will be awarded by the tribunal if the reason relates to trade union membership. Dismissal is also deemed to be automatically unfair if the grounds are solely based on a woman's pregnancy, unless this makes her incapable of doing her job and no other suitable work is available. The dismissal of those on strike cannot be challenged at a tribunal, unless only some of the strikers are dismissed, or some are rehired within three months.

14.4   Procedure on Dismissal

An employer is obliged to give a dismissed employee who has worked for more than six months, the reason for the dismissal in writing if this is requested. This will help the employee to decide whether it is worthwhile pursuing the case for unfair dismissal, provided of course that this option is available and he or she has worked for the required qualifying period (see above) and is not excluded in some other way, for instance by being over retirement age. Should an employee decide to proceed and submit the appropriate forms to the tribunal in time, an ACAS conciliation officer will normally try to settle the matter amicably between the parties if this is possible. The majority of cases are settled at this stage. Contrary to popular belief, if the case proceeds to a full tribunal hearing the likelihood of the employee winning is not very great – less than one-third of decisions are in favour of the employee. (See Section 2.7 for tribunal procedure.)

The remedy that can be awarded to a successful employee is reinstatement (i.e. the old job back again), re-engagement (i.e. being re-employed by the employer but in another suitable post, perhaps because the other is no longer vacant), or compensation. The last option will be awarded if neither of the other two is deemed acceptable by either party, although the amount of compensation awarded will be increased if the employee wishes to return but is not allowed to do so. Compensation is calculated in two parts – firstly as in redundancy (see Section 14.5 below) and secondly as an award to cover loss of earnings after being dismissed. An employee who has immediately found new employment at the same or better rates of pay will thus obtain nothing under this heading. The employee is obliged to mitigate his or her loss and the maximum sum payable at present is £12 650.

14.5   Redundancy

As stated above, redundancy is a fair reason for dismissal. However, it may be unfair if someone is unfairly selected for redundancy in breach of the normally accepted procedures, such as 'last in first out'. Redundancy occurs when work of a kind the employee was engaged for has ceased to exist, or has diminished considerably or because the entire work enterprise is to cease operating or is moving to another base.

Employers considering making workers redundant have a duty to inform any recognised trade union within the workforce and to consider representations made in return. This must be done at the earliest opportunity, but at least ninety days before dismissal takes effect where a hundred or more employees are involved, or thirty days for between ten and one hundred. Compensation may be awarded to affected employees if this is not complied with when it was reasonably practicable to do so. In addition the Secretary of State for Employment must be informed in writing of impending redundancy on the same timescale as the trade union.

Employees selected for redundancy are entitled to the normal period of notice, plus reasonable time off with pay to look for new employment during this time. Those who have been employed for over two years at more than sixteen hours a week (or five years at more than eight hours) and are not over retirement age are entitled to a redundancy payment based on the length of time they have been employed. This is calculated in the following way:

> ½ a week's pay for each year worked in that job over the age of 18.
> 1 week's pay for each year worked in that job over the age of 22.
> 1½ weeks' pay for each year worked in that job over the age of 41 and up to 65 for a man or 60 for a woman.
> The maximum number of years taken into account is 20.
> The maximum amount of pay taken into account is £155 a week (in 1986).
> Therefore the total maximum payment = £4650 (in 1986).

It must be emphasised that this is the minimum entitlement and payments over and above this amount may be negotiated between workforce and management. Where the employer is insolvent, the employees will receive their payment from the state redundancy fund. Redundancy payments were originally introduced in the 1960s to facilitate mobility of labour, but with the onset of mass 'voluntary' redundancies, particularly in the nationalised industries, it is sometimes forgotten that the state scheme only provides a 'safety net' for those not in a strong bargaining position.

An employee will not be considered redundant if an offer of

suitable alternative employment is made and rejected, perhaps as a result of a reorganisation. What is suitable will depend on the circumstances of the case, but simply providing work at a similar rate of pay may not be suitable if, for instance, a loss of status is involved. Where the location of the work is changed, consideration should first be given to whether the employee may be required under his or her existing contract to be prepared to work in different areas, and if not to whether such a move can be considered reasonable, bearing in mind questions of family commitments, etc.

Questions

1 How long does an employee have to have worked for an employer to be entitled to:
   (a) written reason for dismissal?
   (b) a redundancy payment?
   (c) three weeks' notice?
   (d) claim to have been unfairly dismissed?
2 Explain the difference between unfair and wrongful dismissal.
3 What do you understand by the term 'gross misconduct'? When would it be important to determine whether this had taken place?
4 What role is played by ACAS in relation to dismissals?
5 You are the personnel manager of a small company. The following incidents occur, and your advice is sought on how best to deal with them:
   (a) A young employee, Paul, has been verbally reprimanded in the past for use of bad language. He has now sworn at his supervisor in a fit of temper.
   (b) Harriet, an employee of five years' standing, has recently begun arriving late for work.
   (c) Gladstone, a man of forty-five who has been employed as Works Manager for fifteen years, has been off sick for the past eight weeks.
   (d) You are told to make twenty-five people in the machine room redundant.
6 You are a trade union representative and you are approached by the following members:
   (a) Philip who has worked for the company for eighteen months and has been given one week's notice and told he is 'unsuitable for the position'.

(b) Connie who works on the factory floor and has been selected for redundancy with twelve others. She feels this is due to her being an active trade union shop steward.

(c) Kate and Richard, who have been dismissed after five and four years' employment respectively when they returned late to work after a long alcoholic lunch. Richard has found alternative employment, but Kate wants her old job back as she is half way through a management training course.

Inform them of their legal position and advise them of what would be involved in pursuing their cases.

Answering Problem Questions

The purpose of hypothetical 'problem' questions such as questions 8–10 at the end of Chapter 4 is to test your understanding of the law by asking you to apply your knowledge of the formal rules to different situations as you would have to do in real life. Therefore, in order to do this it is necessary to state clearly the applicable rules of law (no credit will be given for irrelevant information, and indeed some may be lost) i.e. the statutes and/or cases involved, with a brief explanation of their provisions, and then relate these to solving the problem in hand. Although these two processes can be done together, it is usually better to separate them as otherwise the answer may become confused. Then to conclude your answer, some advice of a practical nature can be given, bearing in mind the legal position you have outlined. As has been noted in this book, businesses often do not stick to the strict letter of the law, but it is obviously useful to know one's legal obligations before taking up a negotiating stance.

Should you be unable to reach a definite decision on the limited information given to you in the question, do not worry, as ultimately only the House of Lords can give the definitive answer! However, you should aim to advise the parties as to the relative strengths and weaknesses of their positions and the most likely outcome if the dispute got to court. It is unwise to begin your answer with your advice, as it may be wrong and you will spend your time justifying a faulty proposition. Just as with a mathematics answer, the process of analysis which led to your answer is as important as the answer itself.

Table of Cases

160

Table of Statutes

Glossary

Amendment	minor change, not requiring totally new legislation; usually carried out by way of statutory instrument (see Section 1.2).
CBI	Confederation of British Industry, a body representing the interests of the business community, made up of representatives of large companies.
Codification	the process whereby a series of **precedents** relating to one area of law are introduced as one statute to eliminate inconsistencies and overlaps built up over the years, and to make the law more accessible.
Constitution	the set of rules which regulate how a state is governed. This may be 'unwritten' as in the UK and found in a variety of sources, or in one written document, as in the USA.
Defamation	harming another's reputation through the publication of untruthful information, either in speech (**slander**) or in more permanent form (**libel**). e.g. writing, broadcasting.
EEC	the European Economic Community, a body consisting currently of twelve states formed as a trading block and to facilitate trade within the countries. To do so, a vast legal and bureaucratic structure was created.
Indictable	more serious crimes are tried 'on indictment', usually in the Crown Court.
Judicial Precedents	previous decisions of the courts which form the basis of the Common Law system, and are relied on in all similar cases in the future in order to provide consistency.
Judiciary	the collective name for all the judges.
Jurisdiction	the area over which a court has authority to act.
Libel	part of the **tort** of **defamation.**
Litigation	the process of suing in a civil action.

162

Misrepresentation giving false information which induces another to enter into a contract. Damages are sually available for the misled party, or the contract is set aside and the parties put back in the same position as they were previously.

Offeror party that makes an offer – to the **offeree.**

Precedents see **judicial precedents.**

Repeal the process of removing a statute so that it is no longer part of the law. This must be done by Parliament.

Tort the name given to civil wrongs, e.g. negligence, defamation, trespass.

Index